I'M A
GOVANHILL
SWIMMER

Acknowledgements

Govanhill Baths Community Trust would like to thank the following people for their contributions to this publication: all the writers and contributors, the board, staff and volunteers at the Baths, namely Frances Diver, Fatima Uygun, Alex Wilde, Scott Coyne, Jim Monaghan, Olivia Guertler, Bruce Downie, Nadine Gorency, Alan Walsh and Paula Larkin. Additionally we would like to thank Fran Higson, Jon Pope, Brian McGinlay at NORD, Lucie Potter, and all past and present campaigners. We would also like to extend sincere thanks to the Heritage Lottery Fund for funding the production of this publication.

Rebecca Gordon-Nesbitt would like to thank those involved with Govanhill Baths who kindly agreed to be consulted for her text.

Heather Lynch would like to thank all of the people who live and work in Govanhill whose ideas and shared experience has informed this piece.

Rachael Purse would like to thank Karen Mailley-Watt at the Glasgow City Heritage Trust and her ever patient Gary.

Dave Sherry would like to dedicate his essay to the memory of Alistair Hulett and Nessa Mechan – two stalwarts from Save Our Pool no longer with us but who both did so much to inspire all those who worked alongside them.

Govanhill Baths Community Trust is registered as a Scottish Charity. No. SC 036162 Registered Office: 99 Calder Street, Govanhill, Glasgow, G42 7RA

The sale of this publication supports the ongoing work of Govanhill Baths Community Trust.

United We Will Swim

100 Years of Govanhill Baths

Edited by

HELEN DE MAIN

Luath Press Limited

EDINBURGH

www.luath.co.uk

First published 2015

ISBN: 978-1-910745-07-6

In association with Govanhill Baths Community Trust
99 Calder Street
Govanhill
Glasgow
G42 7RA

www.govanhillbaths.com

A CIP catalogue record for this title is available from the British Library.
This publication was produced with the generous support of Heritage Lottery Fund.

Printed and bound by The Charlesworth Group, Wakefield

Typeset in Sabon

Contents

Timeline

1914 On 3 July, the Lord Provost of Glasgow, Sir Daniel Macaulay Stevenson, laid the foundation stone. Bailie Sloan, Convener of the Baths Committee, presided on behalf of the committee. He presented the Lord Provost with a silver trowel. Councillors Drummond and Sadler placed a casket containing documents and other items in the cavity of the stone that was lowered into position.

1917 The Baths were formally opened on 28 February by the Lord Provost of the day, Thomas Dunlop Bart.

1971 The 'steamie' for washing clothes was converted to a launderette.

1998 Glasgow City Council's Sport for All strategy includes commitment to the Baths.

1999 Fears first surface when members of Kingston Swimming Club voice concern that the council plan to close the Baths.

2001 During the first week in January, a council letter about imminent closure 'appears' on the reception desk at the Baths.

15 January – *Evening Times* reports closure plans.

21 March – Community occupation starts at 8.30pm.

31 March – Gala Day held outside the pool on the day of its scheduled closure. Six hundred come to hear speeches, music and entertainment.

10 July – Occupation served 48-hour notice to quit by Sheriff Officers.

7 August – The Battle of Calder Street. There is a dawn raid to evict the occupiers, which hits the headlines and national TV news. A dossier of complaints against police is prepared.

2004 Glasgow City Council announces the Baths are 'surplus to requirements'. The property and land transferred to Development & Regeneration Services for disposal and development. The Save Our Pool campaign applies for

Charitable Trust status in order to reopen baths as a not for profit body and develop a Wellbeing facility for community use – gains backing from Historic Scotland and other bodies.

2005 Govanhill Baths Community Trust (GBCT) formally constituted.

2007 Govanhill Baths Art and Regeneration Team established to develop all aspects of culture and the arts in support of the Baths campaign. Charity Shop on Calder Street opened by Elaine C Smith and MP Mohammad Sarwar. Rear of shop established as GBCT office.

2008 2,192 people tour the Baths during Doors Open Day. GBCT conducts local consultation and research about what people wanted to see in the Wellbeing Centre. Funded by the government, it includes views of over 500 individuals and organisations.

2009 Centre for Community Practice and Trust Offices open.

2010 A three-phase, five-year plan is drawn up for the long-term reopening of the whole Baths building as a Wellbeing Centre:

Phase 1 – the opening and refurbishment of the front suite and working towards the opening of the ladies' and toddlers' pools, an arts space, gardening space, Turkish suite and sauna, gymnasium and healthy eating café.

Phase 2 – the development of the 'steamie' as an events and community space.

Phase 3 – the reopening the main pool.

2011 Charity Shop, renamed the Emporium, moves to new larger premises on Victoria Road. Upcycling 'Rags to Riches' project established.

2012 Formal opening of the front suite of the building. Over 200 attend to hear speeches from Peter Mullan, Nicola Sturgeon and Glasgow councillor, Archie Graham. Historic Scotland approves in principle a £400,000 grant for refurbishment and protection of the building. Big Lottery confirms move of £1,000,000 funding application to stage 2 with £50,000 release to appoint project manager and assist with technical development.

2013 Glasgow City Council replaces one-year licence to use the front suite of the Baths with a long-term lease for permanent use of whole building. Govanhill Theatre Group established at the Baths.

Castlemilk Law Centre opens a permanent advice centre at the Baths. Thirty different organisations book Baths building during the year for various activities.

2014 Learners and toddlers pool temporarily opens. The Prince's Regeneration Trust is appointed as project manager to take forward Phase 1 of the refurbishment the Baths, as part of the Big Lottery funding. Centenary programme of events and activities celebrating the heritage and culture of the Baths launched. Temporary archivist in post to establish Govanhill Baths Archive.

2015 Permanent exhibition of archive collection launched at the Baths, and Govanhill Baths Archive open to the public by appointment and a showcase available to view online.

Foreword

LESLEY RIDDOCH

THERE ARE MANY communities who grumble over council decisions. There are not many who actively oppose them. Still fewer who win – after 11 years of effort. And you can count on one hand the number who succeed with style. Enter, Govanhill Baths Community Trust.

This book traces the epic struggle by local people to stop their beautiful but dilapidated Edwardian baths from being consigned to history when Glasgow City Council closed them in 2001 and advised swimmers to use other pools nearby.

That was never going to happen.

The Baths were one of the few with 'ladies only' sessions, which opened up swimming for local ethnic and religious groups. What's more, people could get showers at Calder Street. There are still homes in Govanhill without a bath.

So protesters occupied the building but were removed that August.

The council thought the campaigners were defeated. They had only just begun.

This book records their long struggle. But it does much more. The building's striking architecture is minutely described. Govanhill's multicultural history is explored. And swimming is put in its rightful historical place – right at the heart of Glasgow's once proud municipal mission to maintain the health and dignity of working people.

The book is studded with memories from local people. Personal, funny and wistful, they demonstrate how a well-delivered, perfectly-located leisure service became the well-loved hub of the Govanhill community. From the 'brick hard' white towels to the hired swimming costumes, women's nights and Turkish baths, this book evokes the heyday of council provision before leisure facilities were farmed out and sold off. It's ironic that Scots excelled at swimming during the marvellous Commonwealth Games of 2014 – precisely a century after the Calder Street Baths were opened – with almost no public pools in the East End today. Just as well then, that the people of Govanhill acted quickly and stayed resolute for so long.

As a journalist with a keen interest in community action, I remember hearing about the sit-in that brought the Govanhill Baths campaign to wider public attention and being struck by the sassy confidence of the protesters. BBC Scotland reported:

> With no swimming pool to exercise in, campaigners went to the Sheriff's offices in the city centre, to keep fit there instead.

Cheeky, provocative and funny – pure, dead Glaswegian.

A few days later Govanhill's 'Save Our Pool' banner was on the huge anti-G8 protest march in Genoa, carrying the message 'Think global – act local'. Internationalist, outward-looking and defiant. Pure, dead Govanhill.

Clear-headed too. Co-founder Andrew Johnson said:

> The [closure] decision was made without a social or health audit in a community that is formally defined in health terms as the most deprived in the United Kingdom, where the chances of dying are 2.3 times the British national average.

Govanhill folk didn't just get angry about that flagrant inequity – they got organised.

Mind you, stopping a closure is one thing. Restoring a very old building during a recession with a team of volunteers – that is something else. And yet slowly, Govanhill Baths has been re-emerging from decades of neglect. Not as a swimming baths fit for Edwardian Scotland – but as a fitness hub for all the community in the 21st century. The building and its original design is still the guiding template however – there will be no flumes.

Since the Baths were reopened in 2012 by actor Peter Mullan, they've been a venue for art exhibitions, theatre performances, a skate-park, and for music gigs. A smart way to keep people involved and the profile of Govanhill Baths high during years of fund-raising, planning and refurbishments.

The plan is to fully reopen the building as a Wellbeing Centre which will help regenerate the area and help boost community health. The Trust is aiming high – all three pools will be brought back into action, there will be arts and cultural facilities, a fully equipped gymnasium, an event hall and a market hall.

With such ambitious but manageable plans, it's clear the lovely old Baths are already working their magic. Govanhill is once again a community on the move.

Far More Than a Swimming Pool

ANDREW JOHNSON

A Beginning

WHERE TO START in the story of a swimming pool? The narrative is stirring, the text simple enough, to omit the wider context would be an act of historical philistinism.

The story of Govanhill Baths is about far more than a swimming pool. The articles in this publication attempt to illuminate and describe the life of Govanhill Baths, with a particular focus on those times since the Baths were closed in 2001, but with a clear light shone on the building of the Baths a century ago.

Against considerable opposition in 1914, Lord Provost Sir Daniel Macaulay Stevenson, with City Architect and Engineer AB McDonald, drove Govanhill Baths (or Pool as it was then known) into being. The Baths represented a philanthropically led commitment not only to improve a community's health, fitness, recreation and swimming skills, but also to challenge the dismal deaths-by-drowning statistics of the day. We can only guess at what was/is contained in the time-capsule which was buried on 3 July 1914, since there is no record of where it was buried. It is likely that it contained a statement of Stevenson's commitment, at a time when swimming was confined mainly to a dirty river Clyde, hot water came from kettles and bathrooms were only dreamed about.

Over the decades that followed, the Baths fulfilled Stevenson's commitment and much more besides, as it became a deeply cherished Edwardian legacy. But, in January 2001, a group of parents from the Kingston Swimming Club (inaugurated in 1892) were offended, indignant and angered by the shoddy and manipulative secrecy of the council. Its furtive operation to close the Baths, under a dark cloak of elective democracy, initiated and catalysed what is now a 14-year-old community campaign to bring the Baths back to life as the Govanhill Baths Community Trust Wellbeing Centre.

In 2001, despite opposition from some councillors, Lord Provost Alex Mosson, with his henchman and council Leader Charlie Gordon at the helm, determined to wreck Stevenson's dreams. On 7 August that year, after a desperate 147-day community occupation to try to save the pool, they had their wrecking way. Eighty-seven years after the Baths opened, they stood smugly and silently by after authorising Sheriff's Officers, 250 police officers (complete with horsemen and whirling helicopters) to ride roughshod over a protesting, dissenting community who had been determined to resist. To the dismay of a grieving community, and ignored by their locally elected councillors, Stevenson's dream was grotesquely, 'eye soreingly' steel-shuttered up by Gordon's privatised agents.

The Past Connects to the Present

The Scottish Government of the day, and its Culture and Social Justice ministers, remained noticeably neutral on the issue and meekly supported Glasgow City Council's dictatorial closure plans.

Anaesthetised, the campaign argued, by its own pomp and power, Glasgow Council refused to acknowledge the tide of community and national dissent that followed.

A bitter ironical historical twist indelibly links these two provosts. The first realised the need to provide essential facilities for a community in need and the second set out to remove them from a community that remained, still, significantly confined to deprivation and hopelessness. Stevenson's philanthropic aspirations and determination that had lasted 87 years were well and truly trampled to ashes with a political and ideological flourish.

This context is all-important because it exposed, the campaign believed, the hypocrisy of those in the council who tried to create a narrative of caring for deprived communities, whilst enacting a careless pretence of anti-racist and equality policies in places like Govanhill.

The past, though, always remains indelibly connected to the present and the future. From that sorry council tale of 2001, phoenix-like, a community resistance from those trampled ashes has arisen in the form of the Govanhill Baths Community Trust (GBCT). Formed in 2005, it determines to pay homage to and protect Stevenson's legacy and the Edwardian heritage he created. Happily the council has moved on and, in general, relationships have healed. The pool has been 'given back' on a long-term lease and local councillors even sit on our Board of Trustees. We are confident that ultimately the 'asset' of Govanhill Baths will be transferred to the Trust.

Top: Exterior of Govanhill Baths, 1920.
Photo courtesy of Glasgow City Archives, Mitchell Library.

Bottom: Lord Provost Sir Daniel Macaulay Stevenson (1851–1944), as presented by Govanhill Theatre Group at Doors Open Day 2014. Photo courtesy of Adele McVay Photography.

A Wider Historical and Political Context

The dissent of the campaign to 'Save Our Pool', though, was not built on some form of romantic political idealism of the far left as some media commentators and councillors tried to argue. Hard evidence existed to show the effects of such a closure in health terms. The Department of Child Health at the University of Glasgow highlighted a battery of research revealing that of the 15 'worst health constituencies' in Britain, nine were in the Clydeside conurbation and the worst six, which included Govanhill, were in Glasgow. The worst of all was Shettleston, which included Govanhill at the time of closure, where the chances of dying under the age of 65 were 2.3 times the British average. It is no coincidence that this concentration of ill-health mirrored the high rates of poverty, unemployment, poor housing and other manifestations of social and economic deprivation.

A few months earlier in 2001 the Scottish Executive had policy proclaimed:

> The best ideas often come from within the community. They know the gaps and failures in services in their area. Service improvement and innovation come best in response to pressure from demanding, informed and confident consumers. To make sure community consultation and involvement is improved across Scotland and that people have a voice in decision-making in their own communities, we are finding new ways to give communities more influence over the delivery of local services.

Thirteen years later in 2014 the Government's Regeneration Committee thundered:

> We believe that strengthening communities' role in the determination, design and delivery of public services can significantly contribute to public services reform and delivering regeneration in Scotland. In terms of its aims to enshrine community empowerment in legislation and strengthen the community's role in decision-making, we welcome the general thrust of proposals set out in the Scottish Government's Draft CE Bill and consultation.[1]

Not much change then, in spite of all the government's continued and recent 'equality' and social justice rhetoric.

GOVANHILL BATHS COMMUNITY TRUST PUBLIC ANNOUNCEMENT

SUPPORT WANTED

Making positive changes within our community requires the endorsement of everyone. The Govanhill Baths Community Trust is holding a PUBLIC PRESENTATION on the future developments of the Govanhill Pool on 18th April. Following this a DROP-IN CLINIC will be held on 22nd of April. You can SUPPORT us by coming along to these events to express your ideas on the future of Govanhill.

PUBLIC PRESENTATION

TUES 18TH APRIL 7-9PM - DAISY STREET FAMILY CENTRE

DROP IN CLINIC

SAT APRIL 22ND, 11AM – 3PM, ANNETTE STREET PRIMARY SCHOOL

Community campaign poster, 2011.
Image courtesy of NORD Architecture.

Can there really be any hope that government and local authorities will pay any serious attention to the idea of a participative democracy or that they will deliver a fair distribution of community resources? More significantly, will it ever recognise the deep significance of Participatory Budgeting (PB) as a vehicle to help grow a fairer democracy? PB is recognised internationally as a way for local people to have a direct say in how, and where, public funds can be used to address local requirements.[2]

The GBCT Wellbeing Centre

Chiming with the highly reputable and influential Carnegie Trust, GBCT defines 'wellbeing' as that which combines health, quality of life and satisfaction. It is about the health of individuals and the whole community as well as the promotion of prosperity.

The Wellbeing Centre we are developing takes full account of those social and cultural needs associated with migration, racism, poverty, inequality, religious hatred, homophobia, welfare, worklessness, ill health and vulnerable people (in general, the Protected Characteristics with the 2010 Equality Act). Therefore, in so many ways, we believe that we supplement and extend the health, social and recreation provisions of Glasgow City Council, as well as Glasgow Life.

GBCT works to meet a fundamental health need within Govanhill, which is one of Glasgow's most deprived areas. Crucially, it is also one of Glasgow's most densely-populated areas, with a highly pedestrianised population, many of whom are recent immigrants with limited English language skills. They simply do not have the capacity or means to travel to their nearest pool facilities at the Gorbals Leisure Centre, and are thus missing out on an essential health opportunity. We want to provide that service locally, so that they can swim, bathe, exercise and integrate culturally and socially in a relaxed environment.

An End? Pipe Dreams, Protest, Resistance and Demands

Will the Carnegie Trust's 'pipe-dream' announced in the same Government Regeneration Committee Report (2014) ever be realised as it urges:

> ... that regeneration strategies are more explicitly linked to improving the wellbeing of citizens in Scotland, and are clearly linked to the National Performance Framework... We see this as part of a wider

Top: Interior of the ladies' pool, 2012.
Photo courtesy of Adele McVay Photography.

Bottom: Interior of the learners' pool, 2012.
Photo courtesy of Adele McVay Photography.

movement towards understanding, measuring and improving the well-being of individuals and communities. Taking a system-wide approach to the overall impact of Government activity can encourage joined up working and help services consider their unintended impacts, as well as those they pro-actively seek, including regeneration?

The British Medical Association has made clear in April 2014 that health inequalities remain 'stubbornly persistent' in Scotland and the Holyrood Health Committee report (January 2015) emphasises 'the growing gap between affluent and deprived communities' in spite of various initiatives and to the extent that the NHS can only offer 'sticking plaster' remedies.

Meanwhile Govanhill Baths sits financially unsupported by either government or council and kept alive by voluntary work and support. GBCT has to 'rent' the Baths building from the council for some £700 per annum on a rolling lease. The lease contains some provision for any major or minor capital works associated with deterioration and we are grateful to City Property for the work it does in co-ordinating these minimal works. Fourteen years of struggle have been littered with fine council and government encouragement, vague suggestions of intent, acres of praise and the tossing of the occasional financial project-crumb (fought over in battles with others).

We are aware that Glasgow City Council has established precedents for large-scale capital contributions for socio-cultural and recreational projects within the council area, and has made provision for similar swimming facilities at Maryhill Leisure Centre at a cost of £7 million. In 2004 the council boasted that the city's compliment of swimming spaces was more than adequate and after the closure of Govanhill Baths there was no need to provide further facilities. Maryhill Baths had been closed for 20 years but in 2006 the council agreed to fund from its own a £7 million leisure centre package that included a swimming pool on the same site, which eventually opened in 2010. Glasgow City Council has also made substantial contributions to the redevelopment of the £9 million refurbishment of Maryhill Burgh Halls, and the £4.5 million refurbishment of Castlemilk Stables and more besides. Why not so in Govanhill?

The story, then, is about far more than a swimming pool. It is about protest, resistance, healing and demands paralleling those of Stevenson and his supporters a century ago when he fought against major opposition to build Govanhill Baths. GBCT will continue the struggle until his dream is given back to Govanhill because it remains as relevant, if not more so, today as then.

We remain hopeful that the council and government redeem themselves, follow Stevenson, and make significant financial contributions towards bringing the Baths back to full health – giving wellbeing a chance!

Notes

1 See www.scottish.parliament.uk/parliamentarybusiness/CurrentCommittees/73168.aspx/

2 See www.pbnetwork.org.uk/ for a resume of Participatory Budgeting and its growth.

BEMA
BEMA
NOT A LIFE PRESERVER

Oral History

I remember the noise: children's voices; kids running, despite the fact that they were told not to run; splashing into the water, making sure your swimming trunks were still secure when you came out again. And being with an older cousin meant he knew everybody here, so I was introduced to people and it was like being part of band or troupe of kids – I wouldn't use the word gang – but it was a great place for exercise and it was just round the corner from my aunt's house.

They were accessible, they were in the heart of the community and they must have been financially accessible, because I never had much pocket money and my cousin didn't have much pocket money, but we could afford to come here without giving it a second thought. So it was clearly physically very accessible and financially very accessible. It was in the community and for the community and, even at that age, as a Glaswegian school kid, you felt you were part of the civic services that were provided.

What I'm also aware of was that it was a democratic institution. I was conscious of kids who were poorer and kids who didn't have what we had – not that we had riches untold – but you were mixing and mingling with people, and I think that's very healthy for society. We've lost some of that.

Neil Johnston

30
Defend asylum seekers

Oral History

I moved up to Glasgow permanently about ten years ago, I got pregnant a couple of years afterwards and me and my boyfriend bought a flat at the corner of Langside Road and Calder Street. One of the things that I was really pleased about was that there was a pool right opposite our house, especially as I don't drive, and starting a family and everything, it's great. And we used to say we were going swimming there and just run across the road in our swimming costumes afterwards, we wouldn't even have to go for a shower. So we moved in in February 2001 and I was going to the aqua-natal classes at the pool at that time. Although I didn't really get to go to that many because the pool shut down in March 2001, I think it was.

My daughter was born at the end of May in 2001, and we took her on her first protest march when she must have been about two or three weeks old or something like that in her pram. And we took pictures and I remember thinking, you know, we'll be able to tell her that when she grows up, that was her first community protest.

Harriet Arthur

The Architecture of Bathing in Govanhill

RACHAEL PURSE

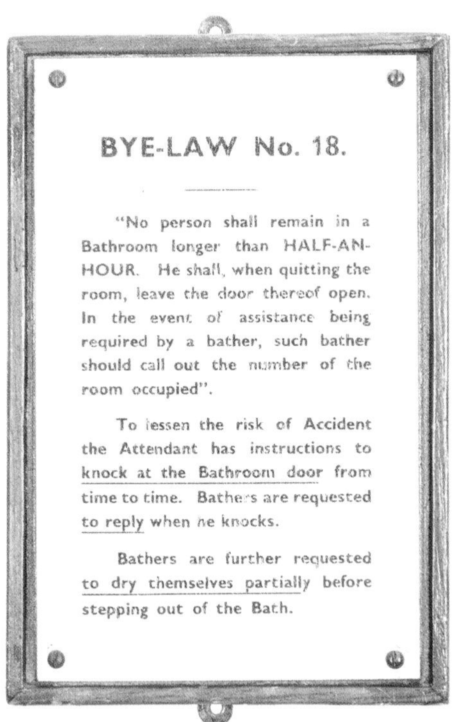

BYE-LAW No. 18.

"No person shall remain in a Bathroom longer than HALF-AN-HOUR. He shall, when quitting the room, leave the door thereof open. In the event of assistance being required by a bather, such bather should call out the number of the room occupied".

To lessen the risk of Accident the Attendant has instructions to knock at the Bathroom door from time to time. Bathers are requested to reply when he knocks.

Bathers are further requested to dry themselves partially before stepping out of the Bath.

THIS UNDENIABLY CHARMING yet unimposing red building is of great historic importance to the city and people of Glasgow. Its significance was confirmed when the Calder Street or, as they are more commonly known, Govanhill Baths were given B-listed building status in 1992 by Historic Scotland. This officially defined the Baths status as a building of regional importance. They are a rare example of a public baths built in the pre-war era, and they were also the biggest public baths complex built in Glasgow when completed in 1917. Govanhill Baths is one of just a few Victorian and Edwardian baths in Glasgow where the building is still in use. For instance, Whitevale Public Baths were hailed as having Glasgow's most luxurious and modern facilities when they were opened in 1902, but the now partially demolished building is in very poor condition, and has been categorised as 'High Risk' on Scotland's Buildings at Risk Register.

Happily, the warmth and passion that locals still have for the squat red building of Govanhill Baths has set it apart from baths like Whitevale, and has secured its future. The story of this building begins in 1914, when the foundation stone for the Baths was laid with great pomp and ceremony in a grimy, heavily industrialised, and densely populated Glasgow. Local dignitaries were in attendance and a time capsule was buried to mark the occasion. However, weeks later, Britain declared war on Germany, and with the country's attention focused on the production of munitions and soldiers, the project was temporarily abandoned. Work restarted without the Baths' original architect, Alexander Beith MacDonald (1847–1915), at the helm. He had died tragically the year after the foundation stone was laid in a tramcar accident in Glasgow. AB MacDonald, as he is known, was born in 1847 in Stirling, but began his career in Glasgow with Smith & Wharrie in 1862. He studied engineering, natural philosophy and mathematics at the University of Glasgow, and in 1870 he entered Glasgow's Office of Public Works headed by Glasgow City Architect John Carrick. Carrick, another architect who hailed from Stirlingshire, was the man responsible for the initial draft of the City Improvement Act of 1866, the Act that led to the establishment of the Baths and Washhouses Committee in 1875, and eventually to buildings like Govanhill Baths being built. The first City Improvement Act was passed in 1865, but the promotion of public health was not yet considered a definite concern of the City Corporation. In 1871 almost a third of Scottish houses had only one room, and it was clear that steps needed to be taken to prevent the spread of disease in Scotland's thriving cities. Councillor William Wilson therefore founded the Baths and Washhouses Committee in 1875, with the aim of providing buildings like Govanhill Baths for the people of Glasgow. The establishment of this committee was a step towards recognising the public health issues facing Glasgow's ever growing population.

MacDonald was made City Engineer in 1890 and a year later City Surveyor. After his mentor Carrick's death, he oversaw the creation of numerous public buildings, including Whitevale Baths, and Ruchill Hospital for Infectious Diseases (1900). The late 19th and early 20th century was a period of great flux for Glasgow as swathes of the city were being transformed in a bid to improve the health of its population. The slums which housed Glasgow's workers were torn down and the city streets began to take on their now distinctive grid-like pattern.

As a visitor approaching Govanhill Baths, it is crucial to be reminded that these buildings were created out of necessity. This was a building fit for purpose. When built, these baths were Glasgow's biggest; and they served the vast local community of working class families by providing them with a place to wash their clothes, cleanse their bodies, exercise, and have a good blether. The Baths quietly opened their doors on Calder Street on 28 February 1917, and were described in a clipping from the *Record* in glowing terms: 'The whole pile really is the last word in baths – public and private.' Glasgow's Mitchell Library Archives hold a wealth of information about Govanhill Baths, including original architectural plans for the building, some hand-drawn. I found this material whilst researching an exhibition on Glasgow's Victorian and Edwardian Swimming Baths, but the jewel in the crown was the personal archive of a Baths and Washhouses Department employee I uncovered. Inside the files I found newspaper cuttings, internal memos, rules, posters and photographs, dating from the late 1800s to the 1920s, all relating to Glasgow's baths.

Opposite: Exterior of Govanhill Baths, 2011.
Photo Gillian Hayes, Dapple Photography.

Overleaf: Interior of the main pool, 2011.
Photo Gillian Hayes, Dapple Photography.

NO DIVING
TO THE LEFT
OF THIS SIGN
DEPTH
1.5m!
DEEP
END
2.06m

Govanhill Baths were the 22nd of their kind to be opened in Glasgow. The Baths contained two swimming 'ponds' or 'pools', one for each gender, as well as a shallower learners' pool. Aside from exercising, a visitor could also enjoy the use of modern 'sprays' or showers and foot-baths. Facilities included a modern shampooing room with great marble slabs on which to lie and a cooling room with 20 beds. There was even a Turkish bath, a sauna, a Russian bath, a cold plunge bath and a cooling room. The inclusion of these facilities in a public building was significant. The corporation was providing its users with the same luxurious amenities as exclusive establishments like the private Arlington and Western Baths Clubs. These clubs did not have large washhouses attached as Govanhill Baths did. There were 68 wash stalls with space for drying at each, and there were 10 large mangles. The overall cost of the Govanhill Baths at the time of building was about £35,000, over £2.5 million pounds in today's money. This serious investment by the corporation confirmed how attitudes had changed since the establishment of the Baths and Washhouses Committee. In a post-war world, laissez-faire politics were no longer acceptable. The Baths remained in use until 2001, with some changes made to the function of the rooms inside, for instance changing the 'steamie' into a launderette in the early '70s.

The red ashlar frontage that faces out onto Calder Street is in the grand Edwardian Baroque style, but its short stature and symmetrical nature, combined with its concealed roofs, give it a welcoming visage, something many municipal buildings could be said to be lacking. The two main entrances consist of a pair of porticos and pedimented door cases. A common stylistic feature of both Baroque and Classical architecture, they make a grand statement, seeming to confirm the buildings status as a state sponsored temple to hygiene and cleanliness. The Classical architectural style may seem at odds with the building's very practical purpose, but Edwardian Baroque was very fashionable in Glasgow during this period, and numerous other public buildings, such as Woodside Library were also designed in this style.

On walking through the porticos, the visitor will notice odd perfectly circular indentations carved into the soft red ashlar of the pediments columns. These are not a strange localised weathering phenomenon, but were created by simply placing a coin flush against the stone and grinding it around and around. These carvings summon up images of queues of people waiting outside, whiling away the time by committing a spot of vandalism. Each hole could be seen as a small community effort, reinforcing not only the practical use of this building, but also its place at the heart of Govanhill.

The overall effect of the facade presents the idea of a stately building in miniature. There are no carvings or decoration within the pediments themselves, but there are rather bulky and now greening vases atop each end of the triangular pediments. Each of these entrances is further decorated with an oculus, or rather a round window, surrounded by a stone laurel. This is again a feature of both Baroque and Classical architecture, but one which here lends itself exceptionally well to the building, giving it a nautical air, whilst also supplying the interior with light. Sitting long and low to the ground the facade of the Baths is somewhat deceptive, in that it belies the scale and size of its interior.

Entering the building, we are introduced to a far more modern and forward-looking Edwardian world, and the focus here is on new technologies and innovations in engineering rather than classically influenced architecture. The vibrant red arches which rise high above both the main swimming 'pond' and the smaller 'ladies' pond' are a testament to Edwardian ingenuity, and remind the visitor of a more famous feat of Scottish engineering, the Forth Rail Bridge, in colour and form. These red supports are in fact ferro-concrete arched ribs, a material commonly found in baths from this period, but few examples from before 1917 are still standing. The ribs themselves are still exceptionally robust, built to last. Up until the 1920s in Glasgow, bathing was segregated by sex. At this point, the desire to swim as a family became more prevalent and mixed bathing was then allowed. Not many public swimming pools can now offer segregated bathing, which is of importance to various religious communities. Govanhill having the infrastructure to do so certainly makes it even more useful to its surrounding community.

High-backed wooden seating surrounds a viewing gallery in the main pool, perfect for watching swimming galas from. The iron on these chairs is painted red, echoing that on the ribs above, and the decorative linear nature of the seating has a whiff of Mackintosh about it. The tiling around the main pool was replaced in the 1980s but the original

spittoons are still in place. To the uninitiated, a spittoon was a small tile bowl which was fixed onto the wall of the pool for the convenience of swimmers spitting chewing tobacco into – very luxurious, as well as unhealthy. The bye-laws poster which I found in the City Archives at the Mitchell Library reminds users that 'No person shall spit, smoke tobacco, or drink spirituous or malt liquors in or on any part of the premises'. The specific nature of these rules can only lead one to assume that the Glasgow's baths were often fairly rowdy and salubrious in the late 19th and early 20th centuries. This slightly raucous atmosphere cannot have been helped by the trapezes and hoops that hung above the main pool. The hoops and trapezes have been removed, although the structure they were attached to is still extant. One can only imagine what a draw this equipment would have been for little boys looking to make mischief, whilst getting fit of course. Two large stained-glass windows bearing the coat of arms of the Glasgow Corporation still oversee the main pool from each end, reminding visitors, boisterous or well behaved, whose pool they were being allowed to use.

The smaller and far shallower children's pool, for the use of teaching infants how to swim, is without doubt forward-thinking. This space shows that the focus within these buildings was not just on hygiene but on health benefits through exercise for the entire community. Whilst in the archives, I found some memos dating from 1908 relating to adverts to be placed on the back of tram tickets in Glasgow by the Baths and Washhouses Department. They give us an insight into exactly what the Corporation thought the purpose of these buildings was, with one advert simply stating; 'WHY DROWN? When swimming provides a pleasant health-giving exercise?'. More specifically, there is an emphasis placed on the education of children in this advert: 'All parents should see that their boys and girls learn to swim, THE CORPORATION BATHS give every facility!'. There is even specific mention of health benefits, as one advert declares 'TURKISH BATH cleanses the skin and defies disease.' Govanhill Baths was built to ensure the health of its users, it was part of a Glasgow-wide crusade against illness and dirt, and this building is a

Opposite: Red concrete ribs and balcony of the main pool, 2012.
Photo courtesy of Adele McVay Photography.

physical reminder of the battle against disease and poor health the Corporation eventually won. It is worth noting, however, that whilst the building of baths and washhouses across Glasgow was a tremendous achievement by the Corporation, the Baths themselves could be seen as a temporary measure for a more permanent and harder to solve issue. The baths and washhouses were built to provide Glasgow's working population with the vital amenities that their tenement homes did not provide them with. However, housing in Glasgow remained an issue well into the 1950s, until modern housing estates containing homes with indoor bathrooms like Easterhouse were built.

Whilst the pools were well used, the slipper baths and wash-house were undoubtedly the most necessary of all of Govanhill's facilities. There were originally 40 slipper baths for men and ten for women, a distinctly unfair division. These so called slipper baths resemble a domestic fitted bath that we now find in our own homes, although they are longer and deeper, enabling the user to have a proper soak. Each bath had its own cubicle, and it is easy to imagine the convivial atmosphere as everyone eased themselves into a hot bath after a long working week, with Friday nights being particularly busy. If you had the time or indeed the inclination, you could also use the Turkish baths, followed by a few minutes in the Russian baths or steam-room. The circuit would be completed by plunging into the cold pool and then resting in the cooling or reading room on one of the deck-chair like beds. This is the same sort of facilities we expect to find in our own, modern, leisure centres, and it is facilities like these, which aimed to ensure the all-round wellbeing of the bath's users. Baths and washhouses built in the early 1900s by the Corporation had caught up with their private counterparts, they were matching them in their facilities and in their architectural design, but what perhaps wasn't taken into account by AB MacDonald, was the people using them.

The archive of our Baths and Washhouses employee contains numerous clippings from the *Glasgow Herald* newspaper which decry the state of Glasgow's baths, with one writer from around 1910 stating that:

> I have lived in several European capitals, but I have never found less attractive accommodation for swimming than in Glasgow... many of the baths are built in impossible slummy districts... There seems to

> be no discrimination exercised in the admittance of undesirable bathers... The swimming baths are utilised for cleansing purposes.

During the first decades of the 20th century, the years in which the corporation built its best public baths, many similar letters were written to editors of papers like the *Glasgow Herald* complaining about the condition of Glasgow's baths, as they were either in a state of decline from overuse or from neglect. Perhaps the corporation was struggling to maintain these vast public buildings under continuous heavy use, demand outstripping supply. The baths, however, were built not for people who had the luxury of spare time for pleasure and relaxation, they were built for the hard-working people who lived around them in their dilapidated housing with no indoor bathrooms. They were built for everyone, and access was for all. Because of this, there were bound to be issues, as our bye-law poster made clear, and as anyone who has grown up in a community will know, there are always one or two 'characters' to look out for. But this is the beauty of Govanhill Baths – this serious temple of health built by the corporation has been filled with laughter, gossip, whoops and screams, and probably the occasional shout. It is a building that has served its purpose well, a building whose place is at the heart of the community.

CITY OF GLASGOW DISTRICT COUNCIL

BATHS DEPARTMENT

RELAX IN A SAUNA

ADDRESSES

Castlemilk Baths (Sauna)
137 Castlemilk Drive, G45 9UG. Tel. 041-634 8254.

Drumchapel Baths (Sauna)
199 Drumry Road East, G15 8NS. Tel. 041-944 5812

Pollokshaws Baths (Turkish)
Ashtree Road G43 1RP. Tel. 041632 2200.

Rutherglen Baths (Sauna)
44 Greenhill Road G73 2SS. Tel. 041-647 4530.

Shettleston Baths (Turkish)
Elvan Street G32 7DF. Tel. 041-778 1346.

Govanhill Baths (Turkish)
99 Calder Street, G42 7RA. Tel. 041-423 0233.

Whitehill Baths (Sauna)
Onslow Drive, G31. Tel. 041-551 9969.

Whiteinch Baths (Turkish)
Medwyn Street, G14 9QL. Tel. 041-959 2465.

Oral History

Turkish baths were something from my culture – as a Turkish person, they were quite an important thing. We'd come here once or twice a week and to have somewhere warm. Fantastic warm place the Turkish baths and, I don't know if you've seen it, but there's a big socialising area, and then the Turkish baths move further and further into the building. We used to take our dinner there, sit in our swimsuits on the sun-loungers and actually spend two or three hours with our friends. Not many places you can do that in Glasgow. So, I was really attracted to that and things like the water aerobics, the yoga and so on and the other things that were offered on women's nights. I didn't come here when it was mixed; I came in on women's nights.

Fatima Uygun

D 00759

GLASGOW
DISTRICT

WASH
HOUSES

MACHINE
SURCHARGE

CONTROL SYSTEMS LTD.

Oral History

I know that when I did live in Prince Edward Street that the woman next to my mother was a regular attendant at the steamie. At least once a week she went down and she had the big high pram and she used to have a galvanised bath in the pram piled high, with washing all tied down. At that time women used to wear these printed cotton aprons, tied round her waist. And she used to have a bandana type thing that they used to tie up their hair with as well, with the same colour usually as the apron. And away she'd go to the steamie in the morning and she'd be away for hours on end. And so you'd see women from all over the area, all making their way to the steamie, with their big high prams, pushing them with the big galvanised baths in them. And the smell from the steamie was just incredible. The washing smell with the carbolic soap, it was big blocks of carbolic soap.

Allan Bruce

A Century of Wellbeing and Health at the Baths

PAUL MILLAR

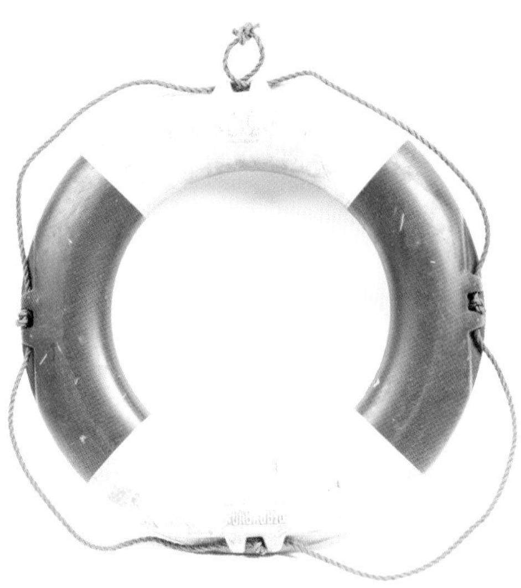

SWIMMING AND CLEANLINESS is surely seen by most people to be a healthy thing. If anyone suggested that being clean and fit was unhealthy they would probably be thought to be mad – or just giving a feeble excuse for their own dirty lazy ways. Sadly, being called dirty and lazy was exactly how many of the 18th and 19th century wealthy people wrote about the poor and labouring classes – and some still do the same today. Many affluent people defended their clean and privileged position in a way that suggested that poorer people somehow deserved the dirt, squalor and disease with which they were forced to live. With profit, not kindliness, as their motivation, private landlords built and let over-crowded flats for most of the poor migrants, without any sewers, running water or washing facilities: then criticised them for the offensive manner in which they washed their clothes or cleaned themselves by swimming naked in the ponds and rivers of the city.[1]

This is the well-known background in which we look at the changes in attitude by the wealthy elite in Glasgow to the cleanliness and health of the working poor. Thankfully, by the 1890s, Glasgow's philanthropically-minded politicians had forced through many public health improvements against the opposition of the wealthy landowning elite. These self-styled 'municipal socialists', as some reformist politicians saw themselves, had only their own humanitarian idealism and revulsion of the squalor inflicted on the working poor to guide them.[2]

Splashing about in water has probably been pleasurable to us from our earliest human beginnings, especially when there was a chance of swimming in warm water. Like a lot of human behaviour, things that are pleasurable and significant to us can quickly become socially ritualised and turned into religiously controlled events. Immersing ourselves in water and cleaning the body became a metaphorical washing away of socially unwelcome attributes such as sins, old beliefs, socially proscribed bodily secretions and whatever else the culture of the day decided was somehow bad, or at least unsociably smelly.

Ritual cleansing in specially built baths goes back a very long way into our past. At Mohenjo-daro in Sindh in today's Pakistan a well-preserved ritual bath is at least five thousand years old.[3] Even today, the thought of someone being 'unclean' means much more than that they could merely do with a wash. Being unclean is as much an idea of being 'seriously unhealthy' than merely being unwashed. Two thousand years after the Mohenjo-daro baths were built, public baths were a central feature of Classical Greek and Roman times. Communal bathing for the Ancients provided religiously important forms of cleansing and purification as well as being very important as a social and business club for the wealthy and influential. In recent times, thousands of years later again, with ancient Roman baths being the model, spa bathing facilities were built in Britain for the fashionable curing of the ills of the rich and powerful and provide a place where they could enjoy themselves.[4] Less affluent people could wash, bath and socialise in their own less luxurious facilities or at least swim naked in lakes, rivers and seas, although often to the horror of 'respectable' society. While washing and swimming were seen as being pleasurable or necessary for health in the baths and spas of the affluent, the uncontrolled wild bathing and washing of the poor continued to worry the sensibilities of Britain's political elite.[5]

Drowning and illnesses linked to wild bathing were a major worry for more enlightened civic leaders who had a concern for the lives of non-affluent people. Humane Societies were founded in the 18th century in response to drowning tragedies. Even today, the World Health Organisation describes drowning as a hidden childhood killer, leading to more deaths among children than either tuberculosis or measles. In Victorian Glasgow, despite the dangers, swimming in the Clyde by working-class boys was very popular on a warm Sunday and the hot summers of 1855 and 1875 were especially noted for busy use of the river. Apart from the dangers of drowning, the 19th century Clyde was also, unfortunately, a general sewer for the factories of the rapidly-expanding city.[6]

To avoid the dangers and public embarrassment of river swimming for the wealthy, private baths were built in Glasgow. These were often based on the ancient Roman bath tradition of hot and cold 'cures' that had survived in the Eastern Roman Empire, adapted by the Ottoman Turks and thought of as Turkish baths today. The motivation by civic leaders to extend access to such baths to the large numbers of non-privileged citizens was philanthropic, as the Glasgow Annals of 1816 state:

> It becomes desirable if not necessary in the interests of health, comfort and cleanliness that public baths should be established for the use of the operative classes of the community as well as for the more affluent.

Top: Govanhill Amateur Swimming Club, *c.* 1980s.
Photo courtesy of John Brownlee.

Bottom: Bobby McGregor awarding Tommy Scott the 50 yards backstroke trophy, 1973. Photo courtesy of Andrew McColl.

These sentiments were added to by Victorian medical experts' encouragement for city councils to help working people to take part in swimming: 'happily, city officials, teachers, and sanitarians are now slowly realising the great improvement in health and temper that comes from bathing'.[7] These ideas of promoting health, comfort, cleanliness and temperament are not at all far from modern ideas of wellbeing. These Victorian reforming ideas came together with other closely related ones in the movements for health, keeping fit and social improvements. Modern sports, gymnastics and athletics became established in Victorian times, including the formation of football clubs, allotment societies and mass political parties with a belief in improving the life and wellbeing of the labouring classes.

The modern concept of wellbeing, though, would have been a lesser part of Victorian Glasgow's concerns for its citizens' health. It is very hard for us to imagine the many health dangers that threatened and frightened Glasgow's citizens over a hundred years ago. When Govanhill Baths were built in 1914, few of us now remember that the building of the Baths was at the end of a massive investment in the health of Glasgow's citizens. The biggest improvement in providing facilities for people's health had already taken place years before the Baths were even opened in the supply of safe water from Loch Katrine in 1859.

In the early years of the 19th century, Glaswegians faced a terrifying number of deadly and debilitating diseases with little hope for effective medical treatment. In 1832, cholera swept through Glasgow causing at least 3,000 deaths in its population of just 200,000, and 1848 and 1853 saw yet more epidemics of that terrible and frightening disease. If cholera was not enough to cope with, typhus fever regularly swept the city in 1831–1832, 1843, 1866 and later. Smallpox, diphtheria, polio and measles were also common and fearsome killers. Influenza came regularly and fatally in the poorly-nourished population of early industrial Glasgow. Typhoid fever was also rampant throughout this time with tuberculosis a common impoverishing and life-limiting disease. These infectious diseases flourished especially among the poor of Glasgow, whose immune systems were weakened by living in poverty and cold, and drinking polluted water. Most of these diseases were spread through polluted water supplies, ponds and rivers. Drinking, washing linen or swimming in infected and polluted water passed these terrible diseases from the sick to the healthy. No-one was immune to this risk, either rich or poor, but the poor were especially vulnerable through malnutrition, lack of sanitation, unsafe water and close contact with sickness in the commonly overcrowded houses. No-one even knows for sure how many took ill and died as there was no proper register of births and deaths in the city until much later.[8]

Even in the late 19th century, there was still little medical agreement about the causes of these terrible diseases. The principles of the hygienic movement were, however, gathering support in political circles. This movement believed in cleanliness as the answer to disease. Getting rid of open sewers and bad smells was the aim, including the promotion of personal washing and cleaning of clothes and bed linen to reduce the spread of disease.[9]

Humanitarian politicians' campaigns led to a long and sustained programme of civic improvements in Glasgow, despite objections by the reluctant private landlords who owned most of the city's housing and who saw little profit in considering their tenants' health.[10] Housing stock was improved by law to provide basic sanitation and washing facilities. By the beginning of the 20th century, when Govanhill Baths was being designed, Glasgow had improved its housing stock considerably. Of 44,345 one-roomed (single-end) flats surveyed, most had their own sink but only 7 per cent of them had their own water closet. In Glasgow's 111,451 two-roomed houses, things were only a little better as only 38 per cent of them had a private water closet. The remaining houses shared common water supplies and toilets. Despite these very basic sanitary provisions, the clean water supplies led to a large reduction of water-borne diseases and a general improvement in health for the working poor. By 1894, death rates had reduced by a third from the mid-19th century, child deaths had dropped by a fifth and water-borne diseases had halved.[11] This was the background of public health success that encouraged the civic reformers and builders of the public baths and steamies in Govanhill and other parts of Glasgow.

Open-air bathing ponds were created first and these were succeeded by more closely-controlled indoor facilities, not merely to provide safer and warmer swimming, but also to suppress the naked bathing by

Top: Clock in the slipper baths, 2012.
Photo courtesy of Adele McVay Photography.

Bottom: *Untitled* by Nikki McWilliams installed in the slipper baths, 2009.
Photo courtesy of Iain McLean.

working men that worried the sensibilities of Glasgow's political classes. The serried rows of clean warm water in slipper baths replaced the need for outside bathing for working families, transforming personal cleanliness and reducing dangers of cross-infection from sick people. The need for cleaning bed linen in cleaner water than the Clyde's polluted riverside was also considered a public health responsibility. Public wash-houses were constructed to let bedding and clothes be cleaned in hot and steamy water, especially to help families when there was enteric sickness in their homes.[12] In this way, washing laundry for Glasgow women was transferred from ponds and rivers to specially built indoor clean hot water facilities – the sociable steamies of legend.

The steamies also changed some affluent people's perceptions of the urban poor as they moved indoors with their washing. It is interesting to read of 19th century wealthy men writing to their friends of the benefits of loafing around on the banks of the Clyde to enjoy the sight of poor women's naked legs trampling linen in great tubs by the river. Inevitably, the sight of poor women washing their family's clothes was also reported as demonstrating their poverty and uncleanliness when the women were actually making a great effort to keep themselves and their families clean with what cold and inadequate facilities they had.[13] The steamie not only restored some dignity to working-class women but was highly valued as a means of keeping their families in safer linen than they had ever been before. All this included the marvellous advantage of exchanging neighbourly chat in a warm and companionable environment. These hard-working and companionable times are still fondly remembered by the former users of Govanhill Baths and the local steamie.

So we can now look back and ask if Govanhill Baths met the health aims of the Victorian designers and social reformers, wondering if things worked out as well as they had hoped. The public baths were a huge success among their intended audience. Working people enjoyed the slipper baths as a normal part of their personal cleanliness as well as the pleasure of exercising in the pools or relaxing in the steam rooms. Sadly, any health benefits arising from these activities must have been seen as so self-evident that little monitoring of their effectiveness ever seems to have been done by the City Baths Department. Swimming became a mass participation sport as going to the baths was enormously popular

Top: Interior of the main pool, *c.* 1920s.
Postcard first printed in Old Govanhill by Eric Eunson.

Bottom: Photo of instructor using ropes in learners' pool, *c.* 1970s.
Found photograph, photographer unknown.

as well as drawing full capacity audiences for swimming club gala days.[14] Basic swimming proficiency was achieved in Govanhill's training pools – a huge incentive if children wanted to swim with the others in the 'big' baths. Baths users could also share and enjoy the millennium-old pleasures of the steam rooms while the steamie reinforced an appreciation of clean warm water, good hygiene and social cohesion. The huge and appreciative response to Govanhill Baths by the community destroys any view that the labouring classes could not appreciate hygiene and the value of safe water. The 19th century 'municipal socialists' proved conclusively that dirt, disease and poverty were not forever bound together. The Baths also rapidly became emotionally owned by their users and they became 'their' baths and steamies. When reforming municipal socialism was sometimes replaced by more rigid municipal paternalism or even bureaucratic authoritarianism, the idea of seeing the Victorian baths as a community resource rather than a gift from governance from above began to take root.[15] The closure of Govanhill Baths in 2001 finally triggered the community to take ownership of this precious health-enhancing facility. In the future, community ownership of health and wellbeing should allow a more sensitive control of just what public health and wellbeing should be for the people of Govanhill.

Govanhill Baths undoubtedly promoted the health of thousands through physical activity and personal cleanliness and thousands more through the facilitation of clean bedding, clothes and fabrics. It is interesting to speculate how many lives were saved by swimming skills taught at Govanhill. Almost nothing of this was directly measured by Glasgow Corporation and the City Council that followed it. If the World Health Organisation is correct in believing that today, drowning is a more prevalent killer of children than some major infectious diseases, then perhaps one or two children a year used their rudimentary swimming skills learned at Govanhill to splutter to the banks of Glasgow's rivers, canals and ponds to live for another day. This author can remember using his 'Calder Street Baths' training to survive the shock of jumping into the cold pools of the River Cart. Over a century at Govanhill and with the contribution of other baths in the City, this could well be amount to many hundreds of lives saved.[16]

Looking back, we can see just how good all this has been to protect the health of communities like Govanhill. It helps to understand how furious the local community was when the Baths were closed. The community's sense of ownership of the Baths saved the building but now the challenge is to return as much of its life-saving, sporting and healthy value to it as possible.

What new health benefits can the Baths provide? Once returned to an active swimming centre it will provide a genuinely community-focused swimming activity. This can return the sense of sociable swimming that is missing in the large modern water-experience pools. The newer large pleasure pools with flumes, wave-making machines and naturally shaped pools do create much of the earlier river and seashore experience that was enjoyed long before civic pools like Govanhill Baths were built.

What the newer pools do not provide is a sense of sporting, community and companionable bathing. The water parks are destination entertainments but not places where we can regularly meet neighbours. Govanhill Baths will provide a local, walkable facility to swim that does not need a car or long public transport journeys to reach.

People wanting to swim should not have barriers to overcome, such as long bus journeys or a need for car-borne affluence. Govanhill Baths can still provide its original function of saving local lives by teaching children to swim. Similarly, slipper baths or showers are still needed in small numbers for those with no easy access to personal cleanliness. Spa and steam-room therapeutic treatments are as wanted as ever and these can include formal hydrotherapy or local access for people needing special assistance to pools. Even public linen washing may have a future in a modern return to the steamie, especially if it is accompanied with a good café and socialising opportunities. Warm companionship in a cold Glasgow winter was the feature most loved about the old steamies.

All these features that promote health and wellbeing, sport, recreation, cleanliness and companionship are as valid today as in the community baths of our ancient ancestors. Health improvements could be much more obviously targeted in a redesigned Baths, especially if there is a continuing trend to the devolution of the NHS to community level. There are possibilities of 'pop-up' clinics, for example, ones especially aimed at migrant groups with their diversity of health beliefs and culturally-defined health expectations. There is some evidence that language and

Top: Synchronised swimmers, 1973.
Photo courtesy of Andrew McColl.

Bottom: Mother holding image of her two daughters, 2012.
Photo courtesy of Alex Wilde.

culture in migrant groups are occasionally barriers to their health, such as with vaccinations and women's health.[17] Pharmacies are moving to provide minor injury and everyday ailment clinics to reduce pressure on GPs. The Baths could provide facilities for targeted community groups to use 'pop-up' pharmacy-led clinics, with translation services if needed. The wide range of health-linked community activities already taking place can be expanded and attract new health-promotion ventures. The Govanhill Baths Wellbeing Centre has been set up to directly explore these possibilities to fit with the diversity of local people. Its existence continues the ideals of the original Victorian designers when the Baths were built a century ago.

Notes

1 Hutchison, I; *Politics and Society in Mid-Victorian Glasgow, 1846–1886*; Unpublished doctoral thesis, University of Edinburgh; Edinburgh; 1974.

2 The belief in the use of municipal control and ownership of the necessities of living for the social and material wellbeing of citizens is best expressed in the Fabian Society writings such as: Webb, S; *Socialism True and False* (Fabian Tract No. 51); The Fabian Society; 1899. A more objective history can be found in: McCaffrey, J; 'Political Issues and Developments' in *Glasgow: 1830 to 1912*; ed. by WH Fraser and I Maver; Manchester University Press; 1996.

3 Kenoyer, J; *Mohenjo-daro: An Ancient Indus Valley Metropolis*; University of Wisconsin; Madison; 1998.

4 Stannard, D; *Bath & Surroundings* (*Insight Compact Guides*); Apa Publications; London; 2004.

5 Glasgow Humane Society, 'Minute Book II, Annual General Meeting, February 1872', cited in, McLellan, D; *Glasgow Public Parks*; J Smith and Son; Glasgow; 1894.

6 Campbell, A; *Report on Public Baths and Wash-houses in the United Kingdom*; Edinburgh University Press; Edinburgh; 1918.

7 Bilsborough, P; *The Development of Sport in Glasgow, 1850–1914*; Unpublished MLitt thesis; University of Stirling; Stirling; 1983.

8 Crawford, R; 'The Struggle Against Preventable Diseases Typhoid and Tuberculosis' in *Annals of the American Society of Political and Social Science*; (1907). Available at www.jstor.org/stable/1010432

9 Knox, W; *A History of the Scottish People: Health in Scotland 1840–1940*. Available from Scran (RCAHMS) at www.scran.ac.uk/Scotland/pdf/SP2_3 Health.pdf

10 Fraser, W, Maver, I; 'The Social Problems of the City' in *Glasgow: 1830 to 1912*; ed. by WH Fraser and I Maver; Manchester University Press; 1996.
11 Butt, J; 'Working-Class Housing in Glasgow 1851–1914' in *The History of Working Class Housing*; ed. by S Chapman; David and Charles; Newton Abbot; 1971.
12 Campbell, A; 1918.
13 Middleton, H (ed); *East End Trail*; Glasgow Women's Library; Glasgow; 2012.
14 Campbell, A; 1918. Swimming galas also seemed to provide an opportunity for casual gambling on results that may have added some midweek betting opportunities when the weekend dog tracks were shut. See Bilsborough, P; 1938.
15 Bilsborough, P; 1938.
16 It is impossible to account for non-drownings as opposed to the more ready counting of unlucky victims. Nevertheless, the Glasgow Humane Society records and unverified reports from the Glasgow Corporation Baths Committees point to a substantial reduction of drownings following widespread teaching of swimming in the City, as much by life-saving by good swimmers as unreported personal self-rescues. See Bilsborough, P; 1938.
17 Scheppers E, van Dongen E, Dekker J, Geertzen J and Dekker J; 'Potential barriers to the use of health services among ethnic minorities: a review'; *Family Practice*, 23; 2006.

ZENITH AMATEUR SWIMMING CLUB

FOUNDED 1955

SEASON 1967/68

Oral History

When I stopped swimming, which would have been about, probably about 19, I joined the committee of the club. I had a meeting with the president and the new treasurer and the vice president and I said, 'Now look, if we want to go forward we've got to get a plan where there is no discrimination.' So we drafted out (I was just told to draft it out) and it was signed by the president that, in future, entry to any teams would be based on ability only, regardless of who you were, where you stayed, or what religion you were. So that was that, we started a system going and we built it into groups where we had the top 36 swimmers in the big pond and it was purely on their abilities to swim. The first month, my cousin moved down into the wee pond. And, I mean, my Auntie Jean was on to my mother, and I said, 'Mother, that's it, if he's not good enough – I can't have one rule for my relations and another rule for everyone else.' So that was that, and there were no more problems about it. In the next four years, we got full control of the club from the beginning of 1971, and the club moved from about 25th in Scotland to 5th.

David Baumann

Oral History

I used to stay in Govanhill in Preston Street. We were great users of the Govanhill Baths. My dad used to take us round there on a Saturday. He was desperate to teach his four girls and one boy to swim. I was just very bad at it. Mind you, when I was at secondary school, we used to go, a big crocodile of kids going to the baths and they didn't have much success either.

My Uncle Willie used to be a swim coach; he was actually a master pastry maker, who worked for the Co-operative. His great love in life was swimming and he did actually teach three of my sisters to swim, but never managed it with me. I was frightened of Uncle Willie and he was the loveliest man really. He had very, very bright blue eyes. Uncle Willie used to coach people. He coached young people who went in for competitions. It was on some kind of national level – whether it was UK or Commonwealth I don't know. I know he had promising swimmers. My sisters assured me they also trained policeman how to swim, so they knew how to get people out of the Clyde. And I remember we found out one time, Uncle Joe came round to show us the paper. 'Look at this, Willie's in the paper!' because one night he had been at one of his training sessions, whether Uncle Willie had spotted it or whether somebody had pointed it out to him, this person lying at the bottom of the pool. And he was the person who dived down and brought them out and saved that person's life. I thought that was so wonderful. I thought the whole world should have known that. I remember I was in that house in Preston Street between the ages of five and ten. I figure I was about nine at that time. It must have been about around 1956.

Wilma Barry

Govanhill – What Makes a Community?

HEATHER LYNCH

> Here we have the paradox, the potentially tragic paradox, that our relatedness to others is an essential aspect of our being, as is our separateness, but any particular person is not a necessary part of our being.
>
> RD LAING[1]

> An outsider, he felt at home with the art and culture of other outsiders, for many years he found companionship across space and time. But from within he came to realise himself as instance of the universal human. The universal human is inclusive and absolute, there is no individual outside it.
>
> TOM LEONARD, A Humanist[2]

WHAT MAKES A community? This question goes in and out of political fashion. The history of Govanhill provides a compelling insight into community, how people live together, manage difference and manage inevitable and ongoing change. This is sometimes anticipated, but most often the result of unforeseen changes in foreign lands, at home and abroad. I was invited to write under the heading 'Govanhill: A Diverse Community' based on my experience of undertaking research in the area previously. However, my own personal history precludes objectivity in my analysis of the area. Govanhill is where I grew up, and where I returned to raise my own children. This view on Govanhill's 'community' is, therefore, as much autobiographical as informed by the oral and published reports of others. The extracts above are perspectives from fellow Govanhillians which speak to their ideas of forming relations with others. In very different ways they report the necessity of human connections in the production of a sense of belonging. This, however, sits in tension with the associated feeling of otherness that connections to 'others' brings. The fluid inter-relationships of 'community', which consist of belonging alongside a sense of alienation, are highly visible in the changing composition of Govanhill's residents at every stage in the history of the area. For the last 100 years, throughout this motion of entangled cultures, Govanhill Baths has been a material constant, central to every facet of social movement, productive in every manifestation of 'community'.

This chapter draws attention to the contribution of the Baths as a material space that has made community a possibility to a changing human population. After a brief description of the different migrant populations who have contributed to the constitution of Govanhill as an evolving, diverse, and often conflicted place, I explore the status of Govanhill Baths as a physical space and social environment that enabled the multi-faceted and plural development of 'communities' in the area. Govanhill Baths 'communities' have much to offer the 21st century as they are not locked by a singular identity but instead provide a space where connections through difference become possible.

Govanhill History – 'Communities' Development

'No Man's Land' is the first documented name for the space that came to be called Govanhill.[3] It was a boggy area that became farmland before transformation into the Borough of Govanhill in 1877. William Dixon, principal investor in the area, had undertaken a substantial building programme driven by the economic buoyancy of the city of Glasgow at the time, which was expanding its borders to accommodate population growth associated with industrialisation.[4] The housing built accommodated workers in Dixon's Ironworks, known as Dixon's Blazes, and their families. The given street names represented Dixon's family and the Dixon Halls, his gift to the people of Govanhill and Crosshill, gives an indication of the value he placed on social relations and cohesion. The Dixon Halls has always been a community space, which has adapted to suit the needs of people living in the area at different points in time.

Some of the earliest residents in these newly built tenements were undoubtedly Irish Catholic migrants as the newly formed Parish of Holy Cross numbered over a thousand before the end of the 19th century. The significance of migration to the area has been present since people first settled there.[5] The evolution of practical and recreational facilities has reflected the migrant waves that have shaped the area's history and social dynamics. Each incoming culture, whether, Irish, Jewish, Italian, Asian or European has contributed to the distinctive quality of life in Govanhill.

There had always been migration between Scotland and Ireland however the 'potato famine' of 1845 left many Irish people without a choice but to seek employment and nourishment overseas. This event, alongside the attraction of employment in the coal industry, attracted many Irish people to Scotland in the second half of the 19th century.

Top: The Parsonage performing at Sonic Soak, 2010.
Photo courtesy of Biotron.

Bottom: Refugee Week, 2010.
Photo courtesy of Lily Reilly.

Glasgow's Southside and its growing industry was a popular place for many Irish people to settle.

The cultural impact is now embedded in the area that hosts a number of Irish pubs as well as two Catholic Primary Schools and a Catholic Secondary School. The impressive Church of Holy Cross Parish and its extensive local membership is further evidence of the lasting impact of this migration.

Italian migrants also came to Scotland in the 1800s to escape poverty caused by drought and unemployment. A number did not reach their anticipated destination in the US, instead settling in Govanhill where they too have made a distinct cultural and social contribution, notably in the form of cafés and restaurants. The renowned ice cream from Queens Café is indebted to the Italian migration, as is the Unique Restaurant in Calder Street, which had a particular connection with the Baths for me and many other people who enjoyed a warming bag of chips after a swim. It has been mooted that Italians may have been attracted to Govanhill's established Catholic community – like the Irish, the Italians endured an often hostile reception from the indigenous population.

A third migrant group to shape Govanhill were the Jewish people who sought asylum from Russian pogroms in the late 1800s and Nazism in the 1930s. Similar to all the migrant groups discussed, Jewish migrants were distrusted and treated with hostility initially before establishing businesses and contributing to the life of the area. I recall a busy Jewish bakery on the corner of Alison Street and Daisy Street that served local people. One of Glasgow's first synagogues was based in Dixon Avenue before moving to its current, bigger, premises on Belleisle Street.

The fourth major migrant movement was from South Asia, involving people from India, Pakistan and Bangladesh from the 1920s through until the 1970s.[6] Initially as cheap labour for merchant ships, those who settled sent word home of the opportunities in Scotland. Much has been written on the historical and contemporary racism experienced by South Asian migrants.[7] However Govanhill was quickly established as home for many South Asians, who made a huge contribution to the economy of the area through small businesses and local shops that continue to serve people far beyond the boundaries of Govanhill.[8]

The most recent migrant group are European migrants who have

Piñata Children's Party, Refugee Week, 2012.
Photo courtesy of Andrew Johnson.

entered the UK on the basis of the European Union agreement to unrestricted movement between member states. This has presented an opportunity for people living in newer member states to relocate in search of better employment. In particular, Govanhill has attracted concentrated numbers of 'Roma' people. Roma were traditionally a nomadic European ethnic group living across the boundaries of nation states. There is extensive documentation of the hardships endured by these people who have been excluded and poorly treated across Europe. In Govanhill their presence has attracted much attention, both locally and from those interested in the status of Roma generally. Like previous migrant populations there are significant tensions that are linked to cultural differences in behaviour and attitudes.[9] Also, like previous migrant populations, the Roma people in Govanhill experience significant poverty that has an impact on their lifestyle choices. The overcrowding and exploitation by landlords who seek to benefit from their economic limitations is well documented.[10]

As a hub of cultural difference, Govanhill has attracted individuals and smaller groups of migrants who are lured by the diverse local amenities, transport links and affordable housing. More than this, despite the long-standing generations of cultural tension, Govanhill is a place that is comfortable with difference. I recall the words of a retired art teacher, recently moved to the area from England. She stated that she wanted to live somewhere that she could comfortably go the shops to buy a pint of milk, if needed, in her pyjamas. Govanhill was a place immediately recognisable as such in its acceptance of all kinds of people. This historical snapshot of the different cultural groups who have influenced the development of Govanhill 'communities' provides the timeline within which Govanhill Baths has stood as a constant, relevant to all, in different ways and at different times.

Govanhill Baths 'Communities'

Govanhill Baths, known to me as a child as 'Calder Street Baths', is a public space which has hosted the diverse range of people described above through different phases of history and numerous points of conflict. In its life as a public bathhouse and steamie from 1914, until its closure in 2001, it made itself available as a space where 'community' became possible.

There was no need to 'plan' or 'develop' community in the Baths, as the space generated the utility, relevance and imagination required to enable people to work, exercise, relax and play alongside each other. It offered a space of co-presence where, on a sensory level, people communed and found unspoken connections. This space of possibility is evident, in my own life experience, and also in the many narratives that I gathered whilst working in the area.[11]

I have strong childhood recollections of going swimming with my friends. At the age of eight or nine, the ability to choose and act independently provided both freedom and a sense of responsibility that we all savoured. The environment of the Baths provided enough structure for us to keep ourselves safe without assuming that, as children, we needed a specific 'youth' space. Conversations with people who attended the pool during the '60s and '70s revealed that more adventurous youths would dive from the balcony railings while the attendant's head was turned.

It transpired that this was a popular activity, which I was advised was best to wait until the end of the session, just in case the attendant caught you. Although there were many reports of pushing boundaries there was also a sense in which people felt safe. Getting 'ticked off' from adults or attendants was part of the experience. Comments from people who attended open days at the Baths in recent years suggested that the space continued to hold this sense of freedom.

The freedom simply to play and explore was not the reserve of the young. Many adults reported the sensation of being in the water – 'lightness', 'relaxation', 'floating', 'buzzing', 'fear', 'freshness' and 'warmth'. These very intimate sensations were experienced individually but at the same time in the context of a collective environment, through the tangible connection of the water. Alongside these individual connections many specific groups were created by people who have different interests and needs, such as women's sessions which provided an opportunity for women who, for personal or religious reasons, did not swim with men. As well as women's, there were men's and gay nights in the very popular Turkish baths. The Baths were for everyone, even people who were not like you.

The Baths naturally created a space where difference was possible. People who used the space moved freely between different groups,

Top: Zenith Amateur Swimming Club Gala, 1969.
Photo courtesy of Andrew McColl.

Bottom: Friends' meeting, 2012.
Photo courtesy of Adele McVay Photography.

without the need to conform to one group identity or another. Everybody was present, old, young, different abilities, sexual orientations, gender and ethnicities. The Baths created a space where people could enjoy splashing, playing, learning and exercise alongside each other, without the need for a structure. An invisible, intuitive choreography ensured that, for the most part, people respected each other's space and right to be there.

Govanhill Baths stands as an emblem for all that is positive about social and cultural difference in Govanhill. This comes to light not just in how people used the pool for swimming, but in how the Baths function has responded to the needs of different people at different points in history. Until their closure, the hot baths were popular with men coming back from industrial jobs; recent Punjabi migrants and, in one conversation, a woman recalled taking a hot bath on the day of her wedding. Bathing would normally be considered an intimate experience and it is testament to the possibility of the Baths as community space that such an expansive group of people, who encompass the range of migrant groups described above, could share this space with each other. The steamie was used by the diversity of local residents until 1971, when it was closed.

There are many stories of hot baths in Govanhill's oral history: learning to swim; using the Turkish baths; attending the Muslim ladies' sessions; orthodox Jewish men's nights; sessions for people with disabilities; mother and toddler swimming groups; Queens Park and Kingston Swimming Clubs. All these stories speak to the affection which people with very different social and cultural backgrounds shared. If this was not abundantly clear when the Baths were open as a functional bathhouse, it came sharply into focus when their closure was announced and has persisted through the last 14 years of campaigning. At the point of closure the multiple interest groups who until that point shared a passive connection, were mobilised into collective action. The unspoken connection that they shared became visible in the swiftness with which people united behind the need to sustain a space that had sustained them.

Interviews by Bernatzky in *Glaspaper* at the time of protest indicate the diversity of people working together:

> I have met so many people, you wouldn't believe. People that I didn't know were my neighbours and whom I hardly spoke to in the past.

> I have never been involved in a campaign like this in my life. It's incredibly creative; this campaign has got housewives, doctors, academics, homeless people, people with drug problems. It's a cross-section of the community life you wouldn't believe and look at this; we get on surprisingly well. I am really proud of people in Govanhill.[12]

Despite the closure of the space, the possibility of people and groups with very different histories, interests and social backgrounds coming together has remained central, to the tenacity and resilience of the campaign. A campaign which continues to captivate sociologists interested in ideas of community.[13] The philosopher Žižek could have been speaking of Govanhill Baths Campaign when he wrote:

> The formula of revolutionary solidarity is not 'let us tolerate our differences', it is not a pact of civilisations but a pact of struggles which cut across civilisations, a pact between what, in each civilisation, undermines its identity from within, fights against its oppressive kernel. What unites us is the same struggle.[14]

My experience of undertaking development work and research in the area lends the authority for me to comment on how the Baths' emblem captured the imagination of these groups. I recall a young group of Roma performers filling the main pool area with their harmonies one open day and the presence of artists is evident in the multiple creative collaborations which have provided the basis for developments such as Streetland, a Govanhill style creative festival. While it may be possible to dismiss the stories of community from decades past as belonging to another era, the collective activity since exists in our current context where individualism is central in other domains of experience. The Baths continues to represent the possibility of a public space. It makes it possible to imagine a community of the future that is not defined by singular identity but by shared experience. The various activities developed by Govanhill Baths Community Trust, The Emporium and Govanhill Grub alongside the variety of arts and welfare activities, appeal to the sensibilities and needs of the diverse and changing range of local people.

Conclusion

It would be naive not to acknowledge the social tensions that have existed in Govanhill, since its transition from 'no man's land' to residen-

What the people say?

A Map of Assets

A Map of Assets study, 2010.
Image courtesy of Neil Maguire.

tial area. Each migrant and cultural group has struggled, alongside the existing population, to establish ways of living together. Despite the undoubted difficulties and hardships that this has created for many, history shows that these tensions have been surmountable. Moreover, the presence of multiple differences has enriched and given Govanhill relevance far beyond its geographic boundaries. The story of Govanhill Baths has provided a central line through this fascination with Govanhill, as a variety of disciplines focus on the area as a means of understanding 'public', 'difference', 'power' and 'community'. Our current moment in history is replete with tensions linked to the troubled negotiation of differences, not only the concerns of migration in the UK but to many global conflicts. There is, I would suggest, much to learn from Govanhill Baths on the successful navigation of difference and the negotiation of the challenges and opportunities this presents.

Notes

1 Laing, RD; *The Divided Self: An Existential Study in Sanity and Madness*; Penguin; London; 2010.

2 See Tom Leonard's website: tomleonard.co.uk/online-poetry-and-prose/a-humanist.html

3 See Glasgow Boundaries Commission 1888.

4 There is much documentation on the Dixon family and their contribution to the development of the area. See Eunson E; *Old Govanhill*; Ayrshire; Richard Stenlake; 1994. Worsdall, F; *The Tenement: a Way of Life: a Social, Historical and Architectural Study of Housing in Glasgow*; West & R Chambers; Edinburgh; 1979. Botti, A; *Making a sustainable neighbourhood: gentrification and urban regeneration in Glasgow*, Unpublished MSc dissertation; University of Edinburgh; Edinburgh 2012.

5 For further information on waves of migration to the area see: Pacione, M; 'The changing geography of ethnic minority settlement in Glasgow, 1951–2001' in *Scottish Geographical Journal*, 121:2; 2005.

6 For greater insight into the South Asian migration to Govanhill, See Audrey, S; Multiculturalism in Practice; Unpublished doctoral thesis; University of Glasgow; Glasgow; 1999. Available at http://theses.gla.ac.uk/4414/1/1999 ThomasPhD.pdf

7 See Bowes, A, McCluskey, J, and Sim, D; 'Racism and harassment of Asians in Glasgow' in *Ethnic and Racial Studies*, 13:1; 1990.

8 Maan, B; *The New Scots: The Story of Asians in Scotland*; John Donald; Edinburgh; 1997. Maan, B; *The Thistle and the Crescent: A study of*

Scottish-Islam Relations; Argyll Publishing; Glendaruel; 2009. The latter source gives an excellent biographical account of the work done in this period by Pakistanis and Indians when they arrived in Scotland.

9 See Poole, L, and Adamsom, K; *Report on the Situation of the Roma Community in Govanhill Glasgow*; University of the West of Scotland; Glasgow; 2007.

10 For current situation, see Harkins, C, and Egan, J; *The Role of Participatory Budgeting in Promoting Localism and Mobilising Community Assets*; Glasgow Centre for Population Health; Glasgow; 2012.

11 Most of the narratives used are from work undertaken with the Arches Theatre (Glasgow) on older adults' memories of the Baths. This project provided the inspiration for Adrian Howell's performance *Lifeguard* which took place in Govanhill Baths in 2012. Other stories emerged through conversations with people in the area.

12 See Bernatzky, T; 'Poolside Conversations' in *Glaspaper*, September, 2001.

13 See Mooney, G; 'Cultural policy as urban transformation? Critical reflections on Glasgow, European city of culture 1990' in *Local Economy*, 19:4; 2004. Sharpe, J; 'The life and death of five spaces: public art and community regeneration in Glasgow' in *Cultural Geographies*, 14; 2007. Jarvie, G; 'Communitarianism, Sport and Social Capital: Neighbourly Insights into Scottish Sport' in *International Review for the Sociology of Sport*, 38; 2003. Mooney, G, and Fyfe, N; 'New Labour and community protests: the case of the Govanhill Swimming Pool Campaign, Glasgow' in *Local Economy*, 21; 2006. Paddison, R and Sharp, J; 'Questioning the end of public space: Reclaiming control of local banal spaces' in *Scottish Geographical Journal*, 123:2; 2007.

14 Žižek, S; *Violence*; Profile Books; London; 2008.

COSTUMES MUST BE WORN
IN THE TURKISH SUITE
AT ALL TIMES

Oral History

It was just a get together, so there was various, there was an ex-boxer who would come, Ogli Tettey, he came from Ghana originally with a guy called Roy Ankrah, The Black Flash. And you'd be lying in the cool room on one of the beds and he'd come in with a big medicine ball, and they are heavy, and he would just throw it of your stomach to waken you up – by god you were wakened up. So he was there, one of the guys was a fisherman and he would cook the fish at home and he would bring it in, a tray full of it and we'd all be sitting eating it. And that one guy brought home-made beer, big plastic bottles of it. So we'd be sitting, television in the background (but we're not really bothered) tea and coffee and big John the attendant. He ran a tight ship there was no anything untoward. He dealt with it, you know, firmly – in his way. An ex-military man so he didn't take any shit from anybody. So, no, it was a great social evening, it set you up for the whole week you know. The craic was very very good, all sort of patter and nobody got above themself – you were all put in your place straight away. But it was a great crowd and really, really missed it when it closed. That was one of the things I missed.

Harry Rooney

Scottish
Socialist
NO WAR
TONY
SHAME

Oral History

There were events at the weekends, quite a lot of weekends, they were outside the Baths, in the street outside. We used to just close the street off and in what is now the peace garden, which is a little strip of land alongside the Baths. So there would be bands, some of the Asian children in dance groups would come and dance – capoeira, the Brazilian martial art dance form, all manner of folk and jazz, all sort of musicians and again drawing attention, ordinary people walking past and saying 'what's going on'. Kids chalking on the pavement. It was a really community thing. I think one of the things was the cross-section of people in terms of ethnic origin, in term of class, in terms of skills, in terms of networking; so many people were involved at so many different levels. I think that's one of the reasons it really worked and people were committed to a particular cause, working together to actually retain this community facility.

Nick Sims

The Save Our Pool Campaign

DAVE SHERRY

History and Context

FROM THE MOMENT its doors opened in 1917 until the council closed them in 2001, Calder Street Baths was a popular community asset. At the start of the millennium it was the last surviving example of Glasgow's early municipal health and leisure provision. Sadly by then the council had closed or sold all its other baths and washhouses.

Concerns first surfaced about Govanhill Baths in 1999 when members of the Kingston Club – the only multi-racial, competitive swimming club in Scotland – feared the council was planning to close it too. Despite official denials and a promise to retain it in Glasgow's Sport for Life strategy, rumours persisted that the real agenda was to run it down and close it.

Donny McFadden's daughters learned to swim there:

> As a parent and a community councillor I worried about its future. At the end of 2000 I was invited to accompany a council officer carrying out a structural inspection. His assessment was that the Baths could remain open at a cost of around £250,000.

The Scottish Council Foundation had just published Insecure Scotland, a report highlighting social deprivation and a chronic lack of facilities in Govanhill. It recommended retention of the pool as a big factor in halting the area's decline. But, in January 2001, user groups learned council leaders had already decided Calder Street would close in two months. There would be no consultation; the Queens Park club for older swimmers found out via a letter left on the pool's reception desk!

Cath Sinclair, representing parents from the Kingston Club, had already raised concerns with local MP David Marshall. He wrote to the council, questioning the lack of consultation and citing many good reasons for retaining the pool. Bailie Liz Cameron replied to him on 11 January, claiming '£750,000 was needed to repair and refurbish' Calder Street, that 'this was uneconomic' given the pool 'was insufficiently used and past its useful life' and that 'Govanhill users would be accommodated at the new Gorbals pool'.

Southside Against Closure Campaign

Parents from the Kingston Club got together with the community council and other user groups and individuals. They held a big public meeting on 17 January 2001, which launched Southside Against Closure (SAC). SAC also agreed to oppose the closure of Govanhill Library.

In *The Glaswegian*, MSP Dorothy Grace Elder wrote:

> Will Glasgow's Swim for Health campaign be aided by closing a top swimming pool? You couldn't make it up, could you? Three swimming clubs will lose out. One has two hundred children and now there's nowhere else to train for competitive swimming in the area. The baths specialise in helping children with disabilities and have special classes for older people. They are very popular and well attended. In line with Glasgow's better health drive there's also a fitness suite and a gym. The baths are one of the few with 'ladies only' sessions, which local ethnic and religious groups rely on. What's more people can get showers at the baths. There are still 100 homes in Govanhill without a bath.

SAC demanded the politicians should retain the Baths, pending proper consultation, but on 5 February a special council meeting ratified the March closure.

Dr Bernie Milligan was a local authority Economic Policy Officer. Interviewed in *The Herald*, she argued:

> Southside population has grown at the same rate that the population of Glasgow has declined. So how can service provision decline in Govanhill with the pool having a catchment area of 70,000 people? It lends itself to lots of different groups. This is an unsophisticated budget saving decision that has been taken without consulting a range of other initiatives in the city, on regeneration, social exclusion and health, for example.

In a letter to *The Herald* Andrew Johnson, local parent, SAC founder member and current chair of Govanhill Baths Community Trust (GBCT) wrote:

> The decision was made without a social or health audit in a community that is formally defined in health terms as the most deprived in the United Kingdom, where the chances of dying are 2.3 times the British national average.

Having steamrollered the decision, council leaders assumed it was all over; they were in for a shock. What Govanhill lacked in wealth, it made up for in community spirit. SAC built mass support through weekly open meetings and launched a Save Our Pool petition that would gather 30,000 local signatures.

Council leader Charlie Gordon maintained that the Baths would close on 31 March and thereafter a feasibility study would be completed. Refusing to meet or discuss with SAC, he now claimed estimates for essential repairs were £1 million but gave no details. In a slick soundbite, he quipped, 'Since the baths are well past their sell by date, SAC can have them for £1'. Peter McCann, solicitor and former Lord Provost, considered bringing a complaint against the council under the Human Rights Act. SAC published a dossier aptly titled 'Sport for Life for Who?' Citing hard facts, key government policies and evidence from professional bodies like Sport Scotland, its demands were simple:

- Govanhill pool to remain open pending full community consultation and a social audit
- Council leaders to meet community representatives to hear their vision for the pool

On Saturday 17 March, two weeks before closure, 600 locals marched from Queens Park to Govanhill Park, calling on the council to relent. MSPs Nicola Sturgeon, Robert Brown, Dorothy Grace Elder and Tommy Sheridan joined the protest, as did MP David Marshall.

Still the council continued to ignore the campaign and for a second time parents lobbied Charlie Gordon at his surgery on 20 March. Again he refused to meet them and spokeswoman, Geraldine Sinkie told the *Evening Times*:

> It's absolutely ridiculous. If the government is trying to promote social inclusion then the local council is going about it the wrong way. In closing this pool there will be a lot of Muslim, Jewish, elderly and disabled people without swimming facilities – a perfect example of social exclusion.

Sit-In or Give In?

Govanhill was not alone. Citywide, the council was closing facilities without consulting local people so Save Our Pool formed a sub-group to discuss direct action. Four years earlier, a victorious workers' occupation at the nearby Glacier engineering factory on Calder Street saved jobs and improved conditions. And, because 2001 was the 30th anniversary of the Upper Clyde Shipbuilders Work-In, occupation was in the news.

Responding to Charlie Gordon's latest rebuff, the angry parents and other pool users agreed that they had to act. On the evening of 21 March they turned up at the Baths.

As Judith Fryer explained:

> We'd been talking about a sit-in for weeks but couldn't broadcast it in case news leaked out. That Wednesday a dozen of us arrived separately at the pool around 8pm, got changed and chained ourselves to the cubicles... We told the manager we were not leaving until Charlie Gordon gave an assurance that SAC could participate in their feasibility study – and that the pool had to stay open during the process. Things went fine. The staff left and the police came and left shortly afterwards, saying they would not intervene so long as we didn't cause any damage. The police and the manager came again the next night to check no damage had been done.

That evening supporters held a candlelight vigil outside the pool. The next day, workers from a local glazing firm handed in £200 and a message of support. From then on food and support was regularly donated by local shops and restaurants and from ordinary people – a measure of the campaign's local standing.

A week into the occupation – with little regard for health and safety – police and council staff smashed through a side entrance using hammers. They drained the pools, cut the electricity, depriving the occupiers of heat and light and turned off the water. They tried, without success, to prevent food and sleeping bags from being handed in to keep the occupiers fed and warm.

Despite intimidation, the sit-in continued, supported by a 24/7 picket on Calder Street. The council's underhand tactics only increased local opposition. The longer the sit-in lasted, the more it rattled the council.

Walkie-talkie radios made communication between occupiers and the picket line easier. It was important to deal with the security guards. Fatima Uygun explained:

> The council hired a security firm but we did a deal with the guards who were on lousy pay. We said 'if you want to keep working and we

> want to keep occupying, we could come to an arrangement. So long as the occupation lasts you'll have a job'. They let us sneak in food and the odd protestor. We increased job opportunities by holding events or threatening to enter the building… The occupation wasn't passive – we occupied other buildings throughout Glasgow to get publicity – like Bellahouston and Whiteinch leisure centres, the Lighthouse and the Kelvin Hall. Later on we even occupied the foyer of the Strathclyde Police HQ because of their intimidation.

Nicola Fisher, a primary school teacher who still lives beside the Baths, was one of the occupiers:

> I came in during my Easter holidays. It was more restful than it was out on that picket line but the council had shut off the electricity and the water by then. We had sleeping bags and slept on sun-loungers. There were lots of people outside on the picket line protecting the occupation. The point was to hold onto the building because we feared the council might demolish it and sell the land for flats.

Support the Occupation leaflets were distributed widely, appealing for local involvement:

> Come and join our 24-hour picket at the occupation. Put your name on our rota for times when you are free to help. Campaign meetings are every Monday at 7.30 in Daisy Street – come along. Every Wednesday outside the pool the community gets together to celebrate the fight to keep our pool open – bring a candle and join our sing-song.

A gala day was planned for Saturday 31 March to coincide with the closure date. On the eve of the event *The Herald* reported:

> Dramatic last minute efforts are being made to save the pool. Scottish Civic Trust said: 'the closure would be a backward step for Govanhill, for the city and for the nation. In the interest of promoting a sustainable community and its heritage assets, we would urge the council to prevent its imminent closure.

Six hundred turned out for the gala day. Calder Street was closed and a stage built for speeches and a concert. There was a barbecue and activities for the children. *Awaz of Scotland*, the Asian magazine, reported:

Top: Save Our Pool gala day, 2001.
Photo courtesy of Nick Sims.

Bottom: Save Our Pool gala day, 101 days, 2001.
Photo courtesy of Nick Sims.

Top: Save Our Pool gala day, 2001.
Photo courtesy of Nick Sims.

Bottom: Save Our Pool gala day, 101 days, 2001.
Photo courtesy of Nick Sims.

After the songs came the speeches and since this was a democratic event there was an open mic for anyone to air their views. They were all sending the same message to keep the pool open. The carnival atmosphere was topped off with the face painting. The kids were walking around with 'Save Our Pool' on their cheeks and foreheads.

The campaigners took their protest to the city's showpiece Art Fair. Carrying placards, they got inside the George Square tent to speak with senior council officials. Judith Fryer told the press, 'To get our message across we decided to choose a high profile event like the Art Fair, for which the council can find the money.'

In the June issue of the *Unison Voice* magazine, a campaigner reported:

> On 9 May the community prevented Glasgow City Council carrying out its plan to enter and strip the building of its equipment, in contravention of assurances that nothing would be removed until the council's feasibility study was completed. The most recent development is that a court order has been served on the occupation. An attempt by the council and Sheriff Officer's to evict protestors is expected at any time.

Eviction Threat

The occupation needed an early warning system because the council was planning to retake the Baths. There were important lessons from the Anti-Poll Tax campaign and from the famous Glasgow rents strikes of 1915, when Sheriff Officers tried to evict families and were thwarted by networks of working-class women – known fondly as Mary Barbour's Army. So SAC created phone trees – networks of supporters who, like Mary Barbour's army, could conjure up large numbers at short notice to defend the occupation.

The Save Our Pool leaflet advised supporters:

> We do not know how much warning we will have. We suspect an early morning raid so keep your phone by your pillow. A lot depends on your early arrival. You will be telephoned and/or text messaged to get to the pool. Bring anything that makes a noise – whistles, horns, and bells. Make a noise on the way to the pool and wear a Save Our Pool T-shirt if you have one. Media will be contacted immediately we

know of any impending action – most of them are on standby for there is considerable interest in this event! Our action is to keep invaders out peacefully and to create a media event. Remember 'losing' the pool, if it should happen, is not the end; it is the beginning of another part of our campaign.

The *Herald on Sunday* revealed the negative impact of closure:

> Donald McFadden tells of a 78-year-old man who lost his wife and didn't know where to turn. He was encouraged to go to the pool and made new friends. Nobody has seen him since the pool closed. McFadden says since the club was forced to shift venue, 100 local children have given up swimming. 'That's an extra 100 kids on the street with nothing to do and nowhere to go. This is more than a swimming pool – it's a centre for the community'. And the community has rallied to the cause. Save Our Pool posters proliferate in tenement windows while local restaurants provide Italian and Indian meals for the protestors.

SAC marked the 100th day of occupation by unveiling its blueprint 'The Future of the Pool – Community support for a Healthy Living Centre'. The following day it held a celebration with 1,000 marching from Queens Park to Calder Street, followed by a street party, featuring live music and entertainment. The event raised £1,000 to defray legal costs involved in contesting the council's eviction order.

Alas, the Court Order was granted and on 10 July Sheriff officers served a 48-hour notice to quit. A determined Nicola Fisher assured the press the sit-in was not giving in:

> We are not moving from this building until the council enters into discussion with the local people. They won't speak to anyone in the local community about the pool. We are here to fight for the community which wants the pool to remain open.

On 20 July, BBC Scotland reported:

> With no swimming pool to exercise in, campaigners went to the Sheriff's offices in the city centre, to keep fit there instead. After that they moved on to the City Chambers to make their feelings known at council HQ.

On 21 July, Govanhill's 'Save Our Pool' banner was on the huge anti-G8 protest march in Genoa, carrying the message 'Think Global – Act Local'. The occupation continued into August, lasting a total of 147 days. Save Our Pool became one of Glasgow's most endearing and enduring community campaigns.

The Battle of Calder Street

Eventually a desperate council ordered Sheriff Officers, backed by hundreds of police, to mount a secret dawn raid, evict the occupiers and seize the building on Tuesday 7 August.

Using excessive force, two helicopters and additional mounted police, they eventually succeeded; but not without a dramatic struggle that captured the headlines and made national TV news. The famous 17-hour 'Battle of Calder Street' saw hundreds rally to defend the sit-in by blocking the roads in a brave attempt to save the Baths. Although police and Sheriff Officers swooped on the building at 4.30am, they could not seal it off until 9.30pm that evening. From early morning crowds gathered around the Baths and protested throughout the day, frustrating the heavy police presence.

Eventually 250 police ringed off the front of the building, allowing workmen to smash the windows and encase them in metal shutters. The 600-strong crowd fell silent in disappointment when the shutters went up. But silence turned to anger as police rushed the crowd with raised batons and mounted police drove adults and children off the streets.

Save Our Pool lodged a list of complaints, including substantial evidence of police racism and assault. Next morning, following a rally and press conference outside the pool, 200 locals marched into George Square to protest at the closure. Singing 'Charlie Gordon's got to go', they handed in a letter calling for his resignation and staged a sit-down protest outside the City Chambers, halting the traffic.

The eviction was a public relations disaster for an out of touch council and Strathclyde Police. Their attempt to criminalise the campaign dragged on into 2003. Thirteen arrests had been made on the basis of fabricated charges; all bar one subsequently collapsed in courtroom farce. The Chief Constable was forced to concede an enquiry into the action of his officers and Fife Constabulary were appointed to conduct it. Their

SHERIFF OFFICER WARNING

On Wednesday 4th July, Glasgow City Council were granted another writ to remove the occupiers of Govanhill Pool.

We need your help to stop any attempts at eviction of the peaceful protestors, the stripping and boarding up of the building.

Sheriff Officers could come at any time. We need you on the picket line and on our emergency response phone list. Turn up with rattles, whistles, klaxons and a peaceful but determined attitude.

We have successfully stopped them a number of times using these methods.

Contact details inside.

GOVANHILL: TOGETHER WE WILL WIN

The Struggle Continues…

Save Our Pool leaflet, 2001.

investigation recommended 18 charges should be brought against police officers but prosecutions were never pursued and the report never made public.

Vast sums of public money were spent pursuing closure – on hiring private security guards, 24 hours a day for 7 months; on policing the 17-hour 'Battle of Calder Street'; on boarding up and securing an empty building; on legal proceedings against the BBC; on pursuing trumped up charges and court proceedings against innocent individuals over a two year period; on Fife Constabulary's lengthy investigation; and on a £15,000 feasibility study, which recommended that the Baths should be re-opened. This entire fiasco cost much more than the £250,000 Charlie Gordon had claimed was needed to keep the Baths open.

In the *Sunday Herald*, Gerry Hassan wrote:

> Police may have evicted protestors from Govanhill pool but Glasgow City Council has a huge challenge. Govanhill is a few miles from George Square, home of the City Council yet the distance in terms of alienation and mistrust is palpable.

The Campaign Continues

Save Our Pool refused to be defeated. To keep the fight in the news it launched a 46-mile bike ride around the city and the daily picket continued until May 2002. Baroness Helena Kennedy contacted the campaign and offered her support.

The Pollokshaws-born QC had learned to swim at Calder Street and she told the *Big Issue*:

> What a tragedy for such a beautiful building – so crucial to the health and recreation of a multiracial community – to be closed down like this. I wish the campaign every success.

Activists maintained the protests, the meetings and the lobbying over the next four years and won increasing credibility and the promise of future funding.

In 2002, a Westminster Select Committee praised the campaign and recommended every effort be made to fund a re-opening. The *Herald* commented wryly on the feasibility study the council had commissioned:

> Andrew Johnson, of Save Our Pool, which battled council hostility and indifference, said it was an insult to local people that a study had recommended a community pool after the council had put so much effort into closing it; 'They kept telling us the building was clapped out and past its sell-by date, yet here is a report saying it is nothing of the sort'.

In 2004, the council declared the Baths 'surplus to its requirements' but Historic Scotland vetoed moves to develop the site and change its use. Save Our Pool applied to become a Charitable Trust and run the Baths on a not-for-profit basis and was supported by Historic Scotland and other groups. NORD architects worked with campaign on a detailed feasibility study and in 2005 the Trust (GBCT) was formed. In 2009, it was granted planning permission for a new Wellbeing Centre.

Eventually GBCT won the building back, raising enough money and backing to refurbish and re-open the front suite of the building in 2012. Two hundred and fifty attended the opening with Peter Mullan, Nicola Sturgeon and councillor Archie Graham as guest speakers.

The campaign was an inspiration, proving what a community can achieve if it stands together and takes matters into its own hands. But the story is not over. GBCT is working towards a full re-opening. United We Will Swim!

SAVE
UR
POOL

Oral History

We heard it was shutting on the first day that it got occupied when we saw all the police and the commotion and what was happening outside. From there onwards that's when I got involved. We used to come down, me and a couple of my friends and that, used to come down and support the people who were occupying it. For us it was a new thing so it was a bit of a buzz, at that age, and when we found out what it was for, it was a good cause. And we got involved, and ever since then I think we used to come every day. I don't think there was a day we missed, up until we got evicted anyway.

It was an excellent feeling. You felt like you were at home, you felt wanted and you felt loved, it was a very good atmosphere out there. Everybody was friendly, everybody got on with each other. I can remember Nessa, she used to come every morning with sandwiches and drinks before she would go to her work. Every day, every morning she would pop by, always with something, she would never come empty-handed.

Qasim Khan

Oral History

I used to love going to the Baths on a Saturday morning early. And I mean early, just after seven o'clock, used to go with Jenny who was my neighbour. She was the girl that was a few years older than me – three, four. And it was Jenny who mostly taught me to swim. The time that we used to be allowed to be in the water, I think was about 20 minutes and then you got the call to come out. But on a Saturday morning, because there was so few people there, sometimes, you got well over half an hour and it was great. You were swimming up and down and jumping in and out, as you wanted. Other days when the attendants were there, they had to be much more strict and they would blow their whistles after 20 minutes and if you didn't come out quickly they went to your cubicle and got off the door – you know if was only a half door – and they'd 'thump, thump, thump' the door until whoever it was to come out, would say 'I'm coming, I'm coming, I'm coming!' It would be about 1933, maybe, 1933, 1934. What age would I be then? Ten, about ten.

Charlotte Murphy

Community Art and the Art of Community

REBECCA GORDON-NESBITT

HOUSED WITHIN A coveted building and providing a nexus through which impoverished and ethnically diverse communities could come together through leisure, Govanhill Baths formed an inevitable target for neoliberal ideologues. When it became known that this valued local resource was faced with closure – after repeated denials by Glasgow City Council – a group of around 80 people began to organise a campaign of direct action and media provocation. Govanhill Pool: Southside Against Closure possessed the organisational skills necessary for the occupation to outlive the sister struggles being enacted around the city; the Baths were occupied and a picket line established to protect those inside. With the odds stacked against them, the stigmatised communities of 'Govanhell' – a term used by detractors of Govanhill, such as media when covering crime in the area or by local racist and anti-immigration groups – with links to Irish republicanism, persistent battles with sheriffs' officers and mounting resentment over skewed planning decisions – refused to be cowed.

Creative strategies were deployed from the outset. Colourful banners, concocted from sheets and spray paint, adorned the picket line. Posters, with bold red graphics on bright yellow paper, proliferated in the windows of surrounding tenements. Children demarcated contested territory with chalk drawings on pavements. A Christmas card was designed and local school children involved. Keen not to replicate the council's apathy towards the community, the campaign group tidied up the peace garden abutting the Baths and painted the railings in rainbow colours. Musicians mutated classic protest songs during Wednesday night vigils, giving rise to a recording and songbook. Music was also a recurring feature of the campaign's other high-profile occupations around the city – at the council's headquarters, the main council tax office, the city centre police station, a well-subsidised architecture and design centre and the annual art fair – the latter in protest at the elite nature of art in privatised public space.

When it became clear that the council could not be persuaded to reopen the building, the Save Our Pool campaign, including Southside Against Closure, morphed into the Govanhill Baths Community Trust, and the Trust shifted its focus onto alternative means of reopening. Antonio Gramsci cites culture as a 'basic concept of socialism, because it integrates and makes concrete the vague concept of freedom'.[1] While various political tendencies – and levels of understanding about the value of culture and the relationship between art and ideology – persist within the Trust, this ethos has prevailed. By the time Historic Scotland decreed that priority in acquiring the building should be given to groups wishing to fulfil its original purpose, the arts had been embraced as an integral part of the campaign. Responding to a call for help, NORD Architects, in association with the Trust, commissioned an Art and Regeneration Study (the naming of which could be retrospectively regretted, on account of the ways in which regeneration has increasingly been taken as a euphemism for gentrification). This document took as its starting point the endemic linkage between cultural activity and urban regeneration to implicate the former in enhancing community ownership of the Baths, with consulted artists expressing an interest in its core activities and surrounding social structures.[2]

Initially attracted to the area by cheap rents, artists involved in various stages of the campaign established Govanhill Baths Art (GBArt) at arm's length from the Trust. Members of the GBArt team invited local artists, culturally active community members and organisations to join them, embracing all art forms and placing the Baths centre-stage in the regeneration activities being coordinated in the area.[3] In September 2009, GBArt, led by artists Lucie Potter, Alex Wilde and Tom Warren, organised an exhibition called Deep Breaths. This included 23 artists, selected through an open call, who collectively articulated an abiding fascination with the building and its contested recent history. A wood and metal construction named after a Swiss architect staked a claim to the main pool; a man and boy, fashioned from newspaper and wire, teetered on the edge of the training pool; a pineapple, evoking those thrown at police during the occupation, was incorporated into a frieze in the Turkish baths. The nationwide Doors Open Day brought in 2,192 visitors to the exhibition over a weekend, temporarily restoring the building to the public and raising awareness of the ongoing campaign. Other events were less well attended, but the significance of arts activities at the Baths transcends mere quantitative measure. The emphasis has always been on quality, as the words of the Art and Regeneration Study make clear:

> Art that is ambitious, recognised critically on a national and international level, and firmly a part of the wider visual art community is

> necessary to this project. This does not mean that only artists of international standing can become involved or that the projects have to have big budgets: it means that the quality of the ideas must be strong, and artists involved must have a degree of ambition for their work in terms of 'positioning' it, locally, regionally, nationally and internationally.[4]

In an embodiment of this spirit in 2010, the 85a Collective hosted an immersive event entitled Sonic Soak.

In 2011, Govanhill Community Action Group was given £200,000 of Equally Well funding to disburse under a participatory budgeting scheme which allows the community to decide how money should be spent. In direct contrast to municipal reluctance, instead of dividing it among the 20 or so groups that came forward, the community decided to give half to the Baths, to develop the front suite, foyer and kitchen. A business plan was drawn up by Scottish historian and social researcher Heather Lynch and the Trust's board, which, along with the funding from Equally Well, secured a rolling annual lease on the building and permission to convert the front suite.

Celebrating the decade-long attempt to restore the Baths to the community, a fundraising auction was held, with works donated by such notable local artists as Claire Barclay, Lorna Macintyre and Lucy Skaer. When the Trust moved into the Baths in 2012, monthly 'Soup, Song and Swally' nights in a local bar brought many folk musicians and the country's top poets together in an attempt to raise money for the campaign – an activity which continues occasionally. At the same time, a concerted effort was made to attract a diverse range of activities. The front suite now resounds with the activities of community groups from Govanhill Children's Choir to Romano Lav (Roma Voices) and the multi-ethnic band, E Karika Djal (The Moving Wheel), which plays mainly gypsy music inflected by Irish and Scottish influences. An upcycling project – Rags to Riches – uses the Baths as a base from which to salvage textiles and furnishings, organising workshops aimed at diverting household objects from landfill.

Skilfully navigating the non-partisanship compelled by its charitable status, the Trust is avowedly anti-racist and committed to the living wage (rather than the minimum wage).Through a process of reciprocal osmosis, the wider ethos of the Baths has permeated into the community. In the cultural field, this has informed three local festivals – Southside Festival, Southside Fringe and Streetland – as well as stimulating the evolution of Southside Studios and contributing to the formation of the Chalet (the latest incarnation of a legendary arts venue known as the Chateau).

Theatre has been a recurring part of the programme since Lynch organised a collaboration with the Arches Theatre which resulted in Adrian Howells' *Lifeguard* being staged with the National Theatre of Scotland. The involvement of Bruce Downie in this production resulted in the displaced Strathclyde Theatre Group finding a home in the Baths. Evolving into Govanhill Theatre Group, Downie's team notably performed an all-female version of *Hamlet* as part of the Royal Shakespeare Company's open stages programme. Reflecting the site-specific leanings of GBArt, other plays have echoed the context of the Baths. The first production *Steaming* resurrected a work in which women from all walks of life come together to save their local bath-house (braving the chill of the main pool in swimwear and towels). In July 2014, Tony Roper's iconic portrait of 1950s working-class Glasgow, *The Steamie*, found its way into the city's last remaining wash-house. In September, a classic piece of agitprop, *The Battle of Calder Street* centred on four key people involved in the struggle, with interview transcripts provided by the documentary-maker, Fran Higson, and poems by Jim Monaghan, Poet and Trust Administrator. Over this period, the agreement between the theatre company and the Trust expired, and both sides seem keen to renegotiate a medium-term deal that will see the theatre company paying the Baths to become a receiving house for touring productions, located in the steamie.

Between 23 August and 4 September 2014, an exhibition entitled *Endurance* – organised as a reference to the longevity of the campaign by GBArt and artists Olivia Guertler and Joanne Neill – included 22 artworks. Alongside those by accomplished local artists Ruth Barker, Ellis Luxemburg and David Sherry was Wolfgang Aichner and Thomas Huber's *Passage* (2011), the video document of a Fitzcarraldean attempt to drag a self-made boat over the Alps to Venice in time for the Biennale. As the exhibition opened, the third Govanhill Baths artist-in-residence was settling in. Ailie Rutherford responded to an open call with a proposal to host a number of discussions over food and drink, reflecting on the next hundred years of the Baths. This process began with a lunch, at which napkins were inscribed with the following questions for guests to pose to their neighbours: 'What will art look like in 2114? How will we communicate with each other in 2114? What will a healthy community feel like in 2114?'

Among the responses elicited, in coloured markers on paper-clad tables, a consciousness of peak resources was evinced and a return to communal living envisaged. Taking account of this soft data alongside artefacts found in the archive, Rutherford plans to fashion future-orientated objects and secrete them alongside their antecedents. Visitors to the archive a century from now will learn that, in 2092, caustic lumps of carbolic soap were transformed into their elegant equivalents, with inbuilt speakers advising bathers of their water allocation in as many as possible of the 52 languages spoken in the surrounding area.

Beyond the part played by GBArt and Govanhill Theatre Group in keeping the building active and the community involved, the presence of the arts at the heart of the Baths conveys the Trust's wider intentions. From the earliest days of the campaign, it has been imagined that reopening the building implies not only the restoration of facilities but also a more holistic focus on physical and mental health. Consistent with these ambitions, the Royal College of Surgeons held an exhibition of health and wellbeing. Despite repeated attempts to deny any long-term connection, engagement in the arts has been shown to have a positive association with physical and mental health, making the work being conducted at the Baths all the more pertinent.[5]

Despite its work for the public good, Govanhill Baths Community Trust remains the only significant community group in the area to be denied core funding by the council. Exhibitions have been organised with neither local nor national subsidy. Occasional project funding has been awarded to GBArt events by the council's arm's-length cultural provider, which, in turn, cites itself as the recipient of (erroneous) accusations that the cultural programme is being funded at the expense of the Baths reopening. For now, the GBArt programme continues to run on goodwill and borrowed time. The appointment of a dedicated arts officer

Top: Mario Botta by Rebecca Lindsay for *Deep Breaths* exhibition, 2009. Photo courtesy of Iain McLean.

Bottom: The Battle of Calder Street, Govanhill Theatre Group, 2014. Photo courtesy of Adele McVay Photography.

is being mooted, but there are fears that this might kill the programme's DIY spirit.

In the meantime, the arts programme at the Baths prompts urgent reconsideration of the role of culture within the community. While the traditional gulf persists between the kind of ambitious, critically received artwork sought in the Art and Regeneration Study and cultural activity instigated by the wider community, the hard edges separating these usually discrete groups have become blurred. At its simplest, the concentration of artists living in Govanhill and engaging in the GBArt programme precipitates a redefinition of community art, defying the low-quality expectations traditionally associated with this term. Beyond this, the alignment of community art and activism, by virtue of shared social, political and cultural goals, houses the potential to achieve 'the kind of democratic and equitable access to the means of cultural production which community artists have claimed as their ultimate aim'.[6]

Notes

1 Gramsci, A; *Philanthropy, Good Will and Organization: Selections from Cultural Writings*; Harvard University Press; Cambridge, MA; 1991.

2 Radcliffe J; 'Govanhill Sporting and Wellbeing Centre: Art and Regeneration Study', commissioned by NORD Architecture for Govanhill Baths Community Trust; Visual Art Projects; March 2008.

3 Govanhill Baths Art, Govanhill Health and Wellbeing Centre: Art and Regeneration Team, 2010.

4 Radcliffe, J, 2008.

5 See, for example, Arts Council England's repeated refutation of the long-term health benefits of arts engagement, discussed in Gordon-Nesbitt, R; *Exploring the Longitudinal Relationship between Arts Engagement and Health Manchester*; Manchester Metropolitan University; Manchester; 2015, and the related evidence base at: longitudinalhealthbenefits.wordpress.com/

6 Kelly, O; *Community, Art and the State: Storming the Citadels*; Comedia; London; 1984.

Oral History

I remember when you went to the baths you got a nice big white towel, but they were absolutely brick hard, because I think they were washed in whatever detergents they used. But I preferred to take my own one in. But you had to pay for a towel and you got a big slab of soap thrown in. Green or pink carbolic, and the smell was nice, but it was like 'hospitally', you know, it wasn't quite what you wanted to smell on the eve of your wedding for a start. And just the smell when you walked in, it was just this hot, steamy, clean smell. It was always really busy, always. You had to sit and wait usually, especially on weekends. And there was a bit for females that I can remember, and a bit for the guys at the other end. And I can remember guys used to try and have a wee sneaky look through to yous. I think it was about one and six, as far as my memory serves me. I think it was about one and six for a hot bath at that time, which was quite a lot of money. But it was well worth it. And if you got to know the attendants, as they called them then, they would let you stay in a wee bit extra. So by the time you came out, your hair was a frizz ball and your face was totally red with the heat and the steam. Just that smell, I can still smell that today. It wasn't a swimming baths smell, it was totally different.

Agnes Nugent

Oral History

When I was very small, and I can't remember the age, it must have been very young, I suspect I was under ten. I came a lot in the early days, largely because it was one of the few places where they would guarantee that no child would leave without learning to swim, at least that was their claim.

Being in the pool with what I thought was a very large and intimidating bloke towing us up and down what I now know is the learner pool – it's really stuck. It's a very strong visual memory that's still there very strongly. And I'm sure he was encouraging us, in a traditional mannish way of 'come along, get moving' and all the rest of it. It seemed a bit scary, but I do remember at that time you basically did as you were told, no matter what it was, 'cause that was what life was like. So I do remember jumping into the pool and straight under the water, and gasping for air, and then being pulled up by this rope tucked under my arms, and then being towed across the water. But, after being towed up and down and half drowning, I suddenly realised to my delight I could actually stay up. I just remember the guy's big grin on his face: 'There you go, son'. He said 'I'm not holding you up any more,' and he showed he was just holding the rope loosely. It must have been no more than four or five pulls up and down the water until nature kicked in and you could swim. And after that, that was it – you were into the big pool.

Paul Millar

Govanhill Baths Archive Site of Collective Memory

MARTHA BROPHY

ARCHIVES HOUSE, manage and preserve the materials created by a government, corporate body, or organisation in the course of its business, or by individuals in their activities. Govanhill Baths Archive is an independent community archive currently in the process of being established and home to material created throughout the Baths' 100-year history. It is a fascinating and truly unique collection which reflects the wide and varied activities and actions which have taken place in the Baths, from its use as a municipal swimming baths and wash house to its occupation by the Save Our Pool campaign and the development of the Govanhill Baths Community Trust.

Anne Gilliland and Andrew Flinn in 'Community Archives: what are we really talking about?' trace the development of community archives in the UK back to local history and antiquarian societies over a hundred years ago.[1] They map this through to a range of working-class, women's, black, gay and lesbian history and archive groups set up in the 1960s, community history projects in the '70s and '80s, and more recently the growth in community heritage and archive activity in the late '90s and 2000s.They discuss key milestones in this recent growth, such as funding opportunities through the Heritage Lottery Fund and 'Listening to the Past, Speaking to the Future' (the Archive Task Force report in 2004).[2] This noted that recent interest in community archiving came 'from a desire by individuals and groups to record and share culturally diverse experiences and stories' and that the materials held by community archives were 'as important to society as those in public collections'. Gilliand and Flinn identify typical reasons why a community (geographical, cultural or thematic) might want to set up its own archive: a need to recover 'hidden histories', a challenge to exclusions in mainstream archives and 'a community's right to own its own memories'. They also assert that community archiving is, 'frequently [a] part of a broader agenda of social justice and political transformation'. Govanhill Baths Archive, an initiative of the Govanhill Baths Community Trust, which grew out of a fight for social justice – the Save Our Pool campaign – fits well into this context.

In August 2014, as part of the Baths' centenary celebrations, I was employed as an archivist on a temporary basis to begin the formal process of sorting, cleaning and cataloguing the material that had been collected so far, creating a basic finding aid (using international standards) and putting in place the structures and policies on which the archive could be developed. The Govanhill Baths Archive began to emerge properly. The materials presented themselves most easily, and with the least cross-over, into three distinct sections: Before Closure (1914–2000), Save Our Pool Campaign (2001–04) and Govanhill Baths Community Trust (2005 onwards).

Most of the materials concerning Before Closure are fixtures and fittings left by Glasgow City Council. There are informational signs for the Turkish baths, the sauna, which direction to swim in, alongside other objects which are quite simply beautiful artefacts that resonate from times past – particularly the large Edwardian brass and hard rubber plug and the cast iron boiler taps – giving us an insight into how the Baths might have looked in days gone by. We have some black-and-white photographs of children being taught how to swim with a rope tied under their arms – certainly not a method used today. More recently there is a 'clocking-in' machine from the 1980s, a life ring and various items of swimming equipment, including common brands such as Speedo but more significantly two 'COG' swimming floats produced by and for the City of Glasgow. These speak volumes about the level of commitment to swimming in the city at that time. People have donated medals and photographs and we are still finding materials from this extensive period hidden in the many disused parts of the building. Recently, blocks of pink carbolic soap were unearthed in an old cupboard in the basement. Although moulding, the sight and smell of these blocks brought memories flooding back for many visitors at Doors Open Day in September 2014. These objects, along with the building itself, provide us with the opportunity to have direct sensory experiences of the past.[3] When coupled with handwritten testimonies and oral histories, which have been consistently recorded since closure, the community has the chance to re-tell its own stories – stories that otherwise would be forgotten.[4] There is growing recognition that, 'knowledge of the past – of a shared history and memory – can provide valuable benefits to any group of people, particularly those who have faced oppression, discrimination and exclusion' as is often the case for the successive immigrant communities in Govanhill.[5]

Lane separator with floats in storage wheel, *c.* 1930s.
Photo courtesy of Tian Khee Siong.

When sorting the materials it was clear that most of what we had dated from 2001 onwards. We put out a call for additions asking the local community if they had anything relating to Govanhill Baths before closure or indeed since. The call was picked up by the local press and we are extremely grateful to Mr Joseph Welch, former secretary of The Govanhill Amateur Swimming Club, who after reading the article donated the hand-written, leather-spined minute book, embossed with the clubs' names, which covers the period 1935–68. He also donated a swimming pool lane separator with floats, and storage wheel, from the same period. These are invaluable and unique acquisitions to the collection. We hope to secure more donations or loans and are particularly interested in photographs swimwear, trophies and certificates – in short, any information that is a record of activity relating to the Baths or the steamie between 1917 and 2001. Glasgow Museums has some material, including the silver engraved trowel presented to Daniel Macauley Stevenson on the occasion of the laying of the foundation stone, which we are able to access through their Open Museums programme.

The materials that were here when I began cataloguing were not here by accident. They were here ready to be sorted, cleaned and catalogued specifically because they were part of Save Our Pool's campaign, to identify and collect evidence to support their call for the Baths not to be closed, to look after the building and its contents during the occupation and to record and document their struggle. The campaign was confident that the city had made the wrong decision and were well aware that the people of Govanhill, in their fight for social justice were making history and that that history, if not recorded by themselves, would be lost. It had a website (launched on the first day of occupation and now archived[6]) and produced many campaign materials including *The Poolside Guardian*,[7] Save Our Pool placards, banners, T-shirts, flyers and posters, a 28-page document critiquing the city's decision to close (published just weeks into the campaign), a protest songbook and CD, letters to local and national government (some with reply), including a letter requesting the resignation of the Lord Provost. Save Our Pool carried out a detailed consultation with former users of the Baths on the impact of closure and what they thought the future of the pool should be. In March 2002, they organised a two-day community conference, Making Waves, which looked at the impact campaigns can make locally and globally.[8] Using photography and video, Save Our Pool also documented the picket, the 1,000-strong march against closure in Govanhill and the demonstration at the City Chambers. In addition, they cut out and collected over 150 newspaper clippings. All of this material now resides in the archive and, like many independent community archives, were collected and saved by a few key individuals in the campaign, namely Frances Diver, Nicola Fisher, Andrew Johnson and Fatima Uygun.

The archive maps the development of Save Our Pool into Govanhill Baths Community Trust and reflects the functions of the Trust with community consultation documents, business plans, architectural plans, annual reports and materials produced by the Trust's many projects: Govanhill Baths Art and Regeneration Team; The Emporium Charity Shop; Centre For Community Practice; and Rags to Riches. It also includes materials from tenants like the Govanhill Theatre Group and external lets like WSREC (West of Scotland Regional Equality Council) who, amongst other things, run cookery classes for the local community. There are exhibition catalogues, poetry books, many many photographs, newspaper clippings from key events, video recordings, publicity materials including the Soup, Song and Swally banner and flyer. Materials from conferences, exhibitions, festivals, theatre performances, music events and much more are now archived. Since the reopening of the front suite in February 2012, the Baths have become a hub of local activity, with around 100 different local and national organisations using the Baths facilities. The archive will house materials which document this use and all future use of the building through each phase on its journey to being fully reopened as a Health and Wellbeing Centre and beyond.

Although the Archive is in its infancy it has already established itself, with the necessary equipment, in what was formerly the sunbed room at the Baths. It has been accessed by researchers for this book, Ailie Rutherford, the artist in residence for the centenary celebrations and Fran Higson, for her documentary film *United We Will Swim... Again*. It has taken part in Doors Open Day 2014 and two primary school visits to the pool. The next steps are garnering further human resources and funding to catalogue the whole collection and make it fully accessible at the Baths and online. It has the potential to become a 'living archive' –

there to be actively used in the present by volunteers and staff of the Trust and the local community for its own education – to gain confidence and a sense of community identity and pride, and to create the future that the community wants.The Govanhill Baths Archive Group[9] has been initiated to take this development forward and in reflecting the aims of the Trust to preserve and conserve the building and advance education, health and well-being in what is a fluid and culturally diverse community, the importance of the archive will become apparent – as Gilliant puts it, 'the organic relationship between a community and its archive [is] vital and central to community wellbeing'.[10]

Notes

1 Gilliland, A, Flinn, A; 'Community Archives: What are we really talking about?', Keynote address, *Nexus, Confluence, and Difference: Community Archives meets Community Informatics: Prato CIRN Conference* 28–30 Oct 2013. The Archives Task Force was established by Resource (now known as the Museums, Libraries & Archives Council) at the invitation of the Department for Culture, Media and Sport, to undertake a detailed investigation and analysis of the state of the UK's archives. Their report, 'Listening to the Past, Speaking to the Future' (2004) is available here: http://webarchive.nationalarchives.gov.uk

2 The Archives Task Force was established by Resource (now known as the Museums, Libraries & Archives Council) at the invitation of the Department for Culture, Media and Sport, to undertake a detailed investigation and analysis of the state of the UK's archives. Their report, Listening to the Past, Speaking to the Future, 2004 is available here: http://webarchive.national archives.gov.uk

3 Prown, JD; 'Mind in Matter: An Introduction to Material Culture Theory and Method' in *Winterthur Portfolio*, Vol. 17, No. 1; 1982.

4 Since Doors Open Day in 2008, the Baths have had a memory book where visitors can write down their memories. This is an ongoing project and each year more stories are collected. Also in 2008, artist Lucie Potter recorded oral histories for her temporary sound installation part of Deep Breaths. More recently Fran Higson, video-recorded testimonies from visitors to the Baths.

5 Jimerson, Randall C; 'Review of *Community Archives: The Shaping of Memory*' in *The American Archivist*, Vol. 73; 2010.

6 See www.web.archive.org/web/20020529052153/http://www.saveourpool.co.uk/

7 *The Poolside Guardian* is the newsletter first produced by the Save Our Pool Campaign and thereafter by The Trust.

8 *Making Waves*, 23 February–4 March 2002, Langside Halls, Glasgow.

9 The Govanhill Baths Archive Group was established in 2014. It is made up of students from the MSc Information and Preservation Management course at Glasgow University, including myself and local residents with a personal and/or professional interest.

10 Gilliland, A, Flinn, A; 2013.

Oral History

Before I got made up to a chan-chan or supervisor, whatever it is, I was a very good swimmer, and a lady had actually lost a diamond ring. The boss came out to me and said 'Joe, can you do anything about a diamond ring?' And I said, 'I cannae do it the now cos there's too many people in swimming'. I said we'd need to wait, I'd need to wait until the kids had blown out the water and the water settles a wee bit, then I'll get my goggles and dive in and see if the ring's on the stank. So I did do this. So we got the kids out and go and get my swimming trunks and dived into the stank. I could stay under the water for quite a while in these days, and I was getting bits of chewing gum and sticking plaster. The first thing I found was a glass eye. I thought it was a ball, I thought it was a marble. So I picked up the marble in my hand. I had a sticking plaster, and I felt the sticking plaster had something stuck on it, it had a bit of chewing gum on it, and it was the ring! So I comes up and says to the guys, 'I'm looking for that'. And the boss at the time, Mr Roberts, he was a great old guy. 'We've got the ring'. He called you son, 'We've got the ring son. That was good. Now away you go and get dried and get a wee cup of tea, and what the hell's this you've got here?' I said it looked like a ball. 'Nah it's no, it's that bugger's glass eye'. There was some guy who used to come in with a glass eye and he was always losing his glass eye. His glass eye was actually missing for a fortnight and I got it sticking on the stank, where it was sticking to a bit of chewing gum. And that was actually what happened. And we used to clean the stanks two or three times a day, with a big 24-foot brush, with spikes on the bottom of it. But the way his eye was positioned, I was just lucky I think in getting it out. And I got the lady's diamond ring at the same time, so I got two for the price of one.

Joe McFadyen

Oral History

Well, I was born on 1 December 1931, up in my granny's front room in 38 Cromwell Road, which is now 38 Niddrie Road. And at the weekend I stayed with my granny, 'cos there was aye someone else getting born in the family. And my uncles, being engineers, had to get washed, and there was only cold water in the house and a toilet, no hot water – that was boiled in kettles, on the range. So I came here with Uncle Ken who taught me to swim and I didn't have bathing costume, and granny said you'll just have to use your underpants and Uncle Ken said no you can hire a costume there. So we went into the cubicle but I wouldn't get undressed because there was a space below the door and I said that somebody would see me, and Uncle Ken said not to be silly. So I got undressed, got on this bathing costume and into the shallow end of the pool. I wasnae allowed out of the three-foot end of the pool and I hung on to the rail and I kicked my feet, and I thought that was me swimming.

John B King

The Future of Govanhill Baths

JIM MONAGHAN

ALTHOUGH THE GOVANHILL Baths Community Trust (GBCT) is still a long way off from achieving the ultimate aim of a fully integrated 'Wellbeing Centre', they have made significant achievements towards this goal. One key element of the importance of the Baths to Govanhill was that it brought together the richly diverse community into a facility that they could share.

Since the opening of the centre in February 2012, the community meeting room, the workshop space and community kitchen have been used extensively by a wide range of groups, reflecting the cultural, ethnic and social diversity of Govanhill. There are 57 different organisations using the spaces. These range from craft groups such as Cast Offs, the weekly knitting and crocheting group, to church groups, such as a Romanian Christian group and a Hindu prayer meeting. A partnership with Castlemilk Law Centre provides much needed welfare and financial advice.

The Trust's own community programme, taking in cooking classes, yoga sessions, the Rags to Riches upcycling project, the Emporium charity shop and other health-related activities, has successfully reached out to the locals, offering many people a step back into their community, building confidence and skills. These aspects of GBCT's activities have recruited volunteers who go on to add to the range of assets and skills we have at our disposal.

However, ticking the box for community use or the sharing of the space by diverse groups is only a small, if significant, step.

The future lies in realising the goal of a Wellbeing Centre, a community resource that caters for the social, mental and physical health of the community. This development will restore the swimming pools and Turkish baths to their former glory, establish a permanent arts and events space in the steamie (the former public laundry), and create indoor and outdoor gardens on the upper floor and roof of Govanhill Baths.

Current in-place funding, mainly from the Big Lottery Fund and managed by the Prince's Regeneration Trust (PRT), will allow GBCT to secure parts of the building, make it watertight and develop the two smaller pools – 'The Teaching Pool' and 'The Ladies' Pool'. The steamie can be stripped out and made ready for its development into an events space providing theatre, cinema, performance and rehearsal space. These steps will enhance the building as it stands for community and arts use, get the community swimming again and greatly increase footfall, participation and revenue for the Trust.

However, despite the generally positive course of events in recent years, there are huge challenges ahead. The financial crash and recession have led to ongoing restrictions in available funding. As community facilities are closed across the country, not only are the funding pots smaller than before, but there will be more competition to secure available funding.

Structural problems in an old building can become more challenging with each year that the larger problems of the building are not addressed. Each passing winter takes its toll on the parts of the building not in general use such as the slipper baths, steamie and main pool. The danger exists that GBCT will be fire-fighting, using the raised revenue to patch up problems as they arise, deflecting from the longer term goal of renovation.

The partnerships that have been formed with City Property (the owners of the building), the project manager's PRT, the in-house Govanhill Theatre Group, and the team of volunteers in various building and restoration skills, leaves GBCT in a strong position to rise to those challenges.

Going forward, GBCT have good reason to believe that they can achieve the full redevelopment of the Govanhill Baths into an innovative wellbeing centre. One of the strengths of the organisation over the 14 years of its existence in various forms is the ability to evolve and adapt. What started as several groups of concerned locals and users of the Baths became an effective coherent campaign group. That campaign developed into a community trust, building towards reopening while playing a full role in the community, providing a range of community workshops and classes and carrying out extensive research works. That highly effective organisation incorporating the Centre for Community Practice had to change again to become a company managing a busy community centre and arts facility. The Trust had to also become a restoration project, finally taking on the task of redeveloping the actual building. At each and every stage in the development, the leaders of the Trust, the volunteers and the community have excelled and shown their ability to keep

Top: 'Cast Offs' at Doors Open Day, 2014.
Photo courtesy of Adele McVay Photography.

Bottom: Collage of future plans for the slipper baths, 2012.
Image courtesy of NORD Architecture.

striding forward, learning new skills, bringing in new people with the necessary skill set and experience. For that reason, they have every reason to be confident that challenges can, and will, be met.

The arts will play a large part in that development. Govanhill Theatre Group and the myriad artists and arts organisations that use the building tend to use the undeveloped parts of the building – the steamie, main pool and 'ladies' pool' – allowing gradual improvements to those parts of the building and much needed revenue from space that would be otherwise unused. This also allows GBCT to promote the use of these spaces, encouraging further use and demonstrating the value of these parts of the building to potential future funders.

There is a lot to look forward to as we enter the second century of the Bath's existence. The unique nature of our community, the mix and range of volunteers and employees, and the continuing success of the campaign against all odds, gives GBCT good reason to think that the next few years will see major steps forward towards their aims. The visionaries who conceived the idea of the public baths a century ago, the people who used the place over the years, and those who fought to save this vital community asset, would be proud of GBCT's achievements. This was, has been, is, and will be in the future, a team effort – a confident expression of community empowerment in action. The slogan that symbolised the campaign in 2001 still, to this day, rings true – UNITED WE WILL SWIM.

Writers' Biographies

MARTHA BROPHY is the pen name of Paula Larkin. She is currently studying an MSc in Information Management and Preservation at Glasgow University. She has been involved with a number of artist led organisations in Glasgow since the 1990s including *Variant* magazine, New Visions and Document film festivals. She has strong family connections with Govanhill and lived here 1988–2001.

REBECCA GORDON-NESBITT worked for a decade as a curator of international contemporary art. Since 2003, she has consistently applied the methods of social research to the cultural field. Her forthcoming book *To Defend the Revolution is to Defend Culture: The Cultural Policy of the Cuban Revolution* will be published by PM Press in spring 2015. She is a founder member of The Centre for Cultural Change.

ANDREW JOHNSON has been involved with Govanhill Baths for over 40 years. He has been a parent of Kingston Swimming Club swimmers, a dedicated campaigner from the outset of the campaign when the Baths were closed in 2001 and, since 2005, the Chair of Govanhill Baths Community Trust.

HEATHER LYNCH is a researcher and artist. Heather has published work that explores material experience of difference as this relates to social policy, gender, ethnicity and disability. She is currently affiliated to the University of Glasgow.

PAUL MILLAR was a town planner for much of his career where an interest in health and the environment led to him to retrain as a health psychologist. Today he enjoys working with health professionals and community groups, supporting and assessing activities that promote healthy lifestyles.

JIM MONAGHAN is a writer, editor and researcher. Former Editor of *Scottish Nurse* and *Medical Network* among other publications in the health sector, he was a parliamentary researcher in the Scottish Parliament. Jim lives in Govanhill where he is Chair of the Community Council and sits on the local Community Planning Partnership board.

RACHAEL PURSE has an MA (Hons) in History and an MSc in Museum Studies from the University of Glasgow. She became involved with Govanhill Baths through including the building in an exhibition she was designing for Glasgow City Heritage Trust. This is her first published piece, and she looks forward to writing many more.

LESLEY RIDDOCH is one of Scotland's best known commentators and broadcasters, with programmes on BBC2, Channel 4, Radio 4 and BBC Radio Scotland. She runs her own independent radio and podcast company, Feisty Ltd, which produces a popular weekly podcast. She is a weekly columnist for the *Scotsman*, *National* and *Sunday Post* and a regular contributor to the *Guardian*, *Scotland Tonight*, *Question Time* and *Any Questions*. In 2013, she published *Blossom – What Scotland Needs to Flourish*.

DAVE SHERRY is a trade union activist and socialist who lives locally and supported the Save Our Pool campaign. He is the author of *Occupy! A Short History of Workers' Occupations* and *John Maclean: Red Clydesider* and *Empire and Revolution: a Socialist History of the First World War.*

About the Oral Histories

THE ORAL HISTORIES featured throughout this book are extracts from longer stories recorded with local people about their memories of the Baths. These have been drawn from two projects between 2009 and 2014 collecting personal stories connected to the Baths.

In 2009, artist Lucie Potter made recordings with local people for her sound installation *Dear Sir Daniel* that was installed in cubicles around the side of the 'ladies' pool' as part of the *Deep Breaths* exhibition.

In 2014, film maker Fran Higson was commissioned as part of the centenary celebrations to document further oral histories with users of the Baths.

The full collection of oral histories can be accessed via Govanhill Baths Archive, or a selection are viewable online: www.govanhillbaths.com

Picture Credits

All photographs are copyright of Govanhill Baths Community Trust unless otherwise stated. Every effort has been made to trace the ownership or source of all illustrated material for the purpose of giving proper credit. We regret any inadvertent error concerning the attribution given to any such material and will be pleased to make the appropriate acknowledgements in any future printings. Please contact us at info@govanhillbaths.com

P12 Kingston Amateur Swimming Club Trophy, 2001. Photo courtesy of Tian Khee Siong.
P22 Orange BEMA armbands, *c.* 1990s. Photo courtesy of Tian Khee Siong.
P24 May Day march, 2001. Photo courtesy of Nick Sims.
P26 Glasgow Corporation slipper baths sign, 1917. Photo courtesy of Tian Khee Siong.
P38 Sauna Advert, 1980. Image courtesy of Glasgow City Council.
P40 Wash Houses ticket, pre-1994. Photo courtesy of Tian Khee Siong.
P42 Life ring, *c.* 1980s. Photo courtesy of Tian Khee Siong.
P56 Zenith Amateur Swimming Club Membership Card, 1967.
P58 Govanhill Swimmers Return – The Gala, 2011. Photo courtesy of John McCann.
P60 Let Govanhill Flourish, 2001. Illustration by Heather Middleton.
P74 Blue Turkish suite sign, *c.* 1980s. Photo courtesy of Tian Khee Siong.
P76 Anti-war street party, 2001. Photo courtesy of Nick Sims.
P78 Save Our Pool poster, *c.* 2001.
P92 Save Our Pool campaign, 2001. Photo courtesy of Nick Sims.
P94 Image of Ruby Brownlee. Photo courtesy of John Brownlee.
P96 Save Our Pool songbook, 2001.
P104 Carbolic soap blocks, *c.* 1980s. Photo courtesy of Tian Khee Siong.
P106 Photo of instructor using ropes in learners' pool, *c.* 1950s.
P108 Govanhill Amateur Swimming Club minute book, 1935–1968. Photo courtesy of Tian Khee Siong.
P116 Goggles, *c.* 2000s. Photo courtesy of Tian Khee Siong.
P118 Interior of 'Ladies' Pool', 2011. Photo courtesy of Gillian Hayes, Dapple Photography.
P120 Save Our Pool badge, *c.* 2007. Photo courtesy of Tian Khee Siong.

GLASGOW CORPORATION TRAMWAYS
(SWIMMING SECTION)
Affiliated with the Scottish Amateur Swimming Association.

Annual Gala
will be held in
GOVANHILL BATHS, Calder Street, Govanhill,
:: on ::
TUESDAY, 29th APRIL, 1924, at 7.30 p.m.

Chairman - JAS. DALRYMPLE, ESQ., C.B.E.
Admission, Adult, 1/3d. (Including Tax) J.C.N. Secy.

GLASGOW CORP
(SWIMMIN
Affiliated with the Scottish Amate

Annual Gala
will be held in
GOVANHILL BATHS, Calder Street, G
:: on ::
TUESDAY, 29th APRIL, 1924, at 7.30 p.m.

Chairman - JAS. DALRYMPLE, ESQ., C.B.E.
J.C.N. Secy.
COMPETITOR.